POMPEI ET HERCULANUM
POMPEJI UND HERCULANEUM

POMPEII
AND HERCULANEUM

Photographs by Jan Lukas/Introduction by Sir Mortimer Wheeler

Photographes de Jan Lukas
Introduction de Sir Mortimer Wheeler

Photographien von Jan Lukas
Einleitung von Sir Mortimer Wheeler

SPRING BOOKS · LONDON

Additional Photography by
Viewpoint Projects and Michael Fox
Research and captions by Howard Loxton
Published 1966 by
Spring Books
Drury House ● Russell Street ● London WC2
© Copyright 1966 Paul Hamlyn Ltd
Printed in Czechoslovakia by Svoboda, Prague
T 1706

Contents
Table des Matières
Inhalt

Colour Plates

Photos en Couleurs

Farbphotographien

Frontispiece:
The Via di Mercurio, seen from the Torre di Mercurio. The Forum can just be seen at the far end of the street

Photograph by Van Phillips

Frontispice:
La Via di Mercurio, vue de la Torre di Mercurio. D'ici le Forum se rend visible au bout de la rue

Titelbild:
Die Via di Mercurio vom Torre di Mercurio gesehen. Das Forum steht am Strassenende

Page 15:
Wall painting from the House of the Vetii

Photograph by Denis Hughes-Gilbey

Page 15:
Peinture murale dans la Maison des Vetii

Seite 15:
Wandmalerei im Hause der Vettier

Page 16:
The Forum

Photograph by A. F. Kersting

Page 16:
Le Forum

Seite 16:
Das Forum

Introduction

Anciently, as today, the Greek city of Neapolis or Naples looked southward to a curving coastline marked by little towns linked by a scatter of farms and country-houses. The limit of the vista is Capri, with its sinister landward bluff and its almost legendary emperor Tiberius; but underlying the Romanized and modernized landscape of the mainland there remains something more than a memory of the Hellenic colonists who first civilized its native Oscans and prepared the way for ultimate Roman dominion. The town-plan of Neapolis, as we know it, and those of Pompeii and Herculaneum (the Greek Herakleia or Herakleion), with their elongated blocks or *insulae*, have their analogues in Greek cities such as Olynthus. Here basically is a limb of the Greek world, even though in substance there is little now that is Greek upon the surface. The photographs assembled in this book show us mostly the Roman overlay dating from the first centuries B.C. and A.D.

Of Pompeii and Herculaneum it can fairly be said that nothing in their life became them like the leaving it. And by the grace of fortune the story of their departure in the fatal year A.D. 79 is graven in literature by one who himself saw the circumstance; by the younger Pliny whose uncle the Naturalist, a man of infinite curiosity and erudition, perished whilst observing and recording the mighty conflagration. The nephew described the scene shortly afterwards in a famous letter to his friend, the historian Tacitus.

At about one o'clock in the afternoon of the 24th August the narrator's mother drew his uncle's attention to a cloud which suddenly darkened the skies of the Bay of Naples and was found afterwards to issue from the crater of Vesuvius. It resembled, we are told, a fir-tree with a tall trunk which spread at the top into a number of branches, at one moment white, at another dark and spotted as though it carried earth and cinders. The elder Pliny, who was in command of a fleet near Naples, launched his galleys and sailed towards the scene of the disaster to investigate and to help, plainly without any clear idea of the nature of the need. He went ashore at Stabiae, south of Pompeii, withdrew to a friend's house, and bathed and "dined with real or assumed cheerfulness". Falling pumice-stones and ashes disturbed the subsequent sleep of the household; and in the morning the learned but manifestly rather futile old gentleman lay stifled upon the beach.

Since then the last days of Pompeii have been elaborated by Lord Lytton and, above all, by the excavators who, since the 18th century, have carved out an appreciable part of the Roman town from the thick layer of lava and consolidated ashes that simultaneously buried it and preserved it in an infinitude of detail. Here on a table lay the half-eaten dinner of eggs and fish and nuts which the priests of Isis had left precipitately in a vain attempt to save their temple treasures. There in a tomb outside the town-walls a family had been celebrating a funeral feast when the door of the chapel was blocked by lava and the celebrants were imprisoned in death. Elsewhere, wine-jars and mugs still stood ready within the tavern, and loose change remained in the till. A chained dog, forgotten in the panic, had perished in its struggles. Equally forgotten lay two manacled prisoners in the barracks of the gladiators, near the amphitheatre. In another room of the barracks, amidst a heap of skeletons, was that of a woman wearing splendid jewellery — and archaeological tittle-tattle has not been idle. Elsewhere again, the corpse of a woman clasped a baby, whilst two small girls were clinging to her dress. And so on. These and many other Pompeiians, beaten down by burning ashes or asphyxiated by fumes, had been perpetuated as cavities in the encompassing lava and have been recovered with astonishing completeness by the process of pouring liquid plaster into the iron-hard moulds. In their cheerless way these plaster images bring vividly to life again the inhabitants, slave and free, of the doomed city.

But be it admitted that, apart from these macabre relics, now confined to museums, there is today a strange melancholy about the place itself. Excavated streets, shops and houses, many in working-order, give it a sense alike of actuality and of sinister emptiness, which hordes of alien tourists serve merely to emphasize. Real and relevant life had indeed forever ceased there at one o'clock on that August day.

Only once in many visits have I felt attuned to all this dereliction. On the evening of the 30th September, 1943, my military caravan had been driven into the shelter of the Amphitheatre Gate as far as a new bomb-crater would permit. Now and then the flash of a gun or the leisurely whine of a mortar-shell broke the gathering night. High up in the darkness the inflamed eye of the volcano — it was appropriately active that year — blinked beneath the Plough. In the privacy of dawn I walked briefly across to the New Excavations where, thanks to careful technique, the houses stood once more roof-high, lining the Roman street with astonishing verisimilitude in the half-light. Indeed, so convincing were they that, by understandable error, they had recently been bombed from the air, and the atmosphere still bore the taint of high-explosive. The moment was apt. For an instant in this second death the whole street came alive . . .

Perhaps the most eloquent traces of the 'man in the street' at Pompeii are the notices and casual scribblings on the plastered house-walls. These graffiti are in fact almost a cultural cross-section of the population. Many hundreds of them are election notices, some of amateur appearance but others evidently painted by skilled professionals. Indeed one of these professionals names himself, and his house is conveniently identified for his clients by the painted notice outside it that 'Aemilius Celer lives here'. The notices may be content to describe their candidate as 'a good man'; but others go further and state that he is 'a trustworthy young man', or 'a young man of unimpeachable modesty'. Of one it is promised that 'he will carefully safeguard the public purse'. Another advertisement says 'Proculus, make Sabinus aedile, and he will do as much for you'. Opposition posters weigh in with the information that 'the thieves ask you to make Vatia aedile'; another states that 'all the drunkards and sleepers' back the same unfortunate Vatia. More charmingly, Claudius is commended for the office of mayor by 'his sweetheart'.

Then there are notices of forthcoming gladiatorial shows, and others of properties for sale or renting; one property is described as 'fit for a knight'. Less formal scrawls include, as today, the names of idlers, sometimes with an added message such as 'go and hang yourself'. Love is naturally a frequent theme; summed up in someone's advice 'no one is a gentleman who has not loved a woman'. The passerby is also warned that 'Restitutus has often deceived many girls'. But amongst all this perennial persiflage it is of interest to observe many quotations from the poets;

Vergil, Ovid, Propertius, Lucretius are amongst those identified. The universal literacy of the Pompeiian man in the street is sufficiently evident, and the memorization of poetry is implied as a normal part of his education.

It is probably significant that, whilst the walls of Pompeii are covered with political slogans, personalities and ruderies, those of Herculaneum, 9 miles up the coast towards Naples, remain almost entirely unsullied, so far as we know them. There are other evidences that Herculaneum, less than a third of the size of Pompeii, filled a different and socially superior function. Pompeii contained men of some wealth but was essentially a middle-class commercial town. Herculaneum too had its trading element but — at any rate until the disastrous earthquake which shook the whole coast in A.D. 63 — this was subordinate to a prosperous community of educated folk who chose to live in comfortable porticoed mansions upon a carefully chosen seaward slope, with terraces and belvederes appropriate to an Augustan sensibility.

Unlike Pompeii, which was buried beneath ashes and lava, Herculaneum was overwhelmed by a vast torrent of volcanic mud. This mud-stream and its effect are best observed by the visitor in the Suburban or Shore baths, one of the more recently excavated structures.[1] Here the mud has vividly preserved wooden doors and other fittings dislodged by the impact. Incidentally, the building is also notable architecturally for the imposition of arches directly on columns in a fashion which did

not become normal until later Roman times.

Of the four blocks or insulae laid bare, one is devoted to other public baths of the kind which formed a popular social rendezvous in all Roman towns. For the rest, each insula contains either one or two substantial houses, often with wall-paintings and sculptures of considerable interest, and sometimes with a terraced garden of some pretension. Cheek-by-jowl with these mansions are smaller houses, not infrequently associated with shops and workshops in a democratic neighbourliness that recurs at Pompeii, and at Herculaneum may represent a lowering of standards after the great earthquake. The appearance of tall tenement-buildings on the fringe of the excavated site points in a similar direction: the crowding in of a considerable lower-grade population in the last phase of the town and the consequent need (exactly as in our modern cities) to build higher within an increasingly inadequate and valuable ground-space.

One large house which was subdivided to accommodate a number of families in this late phase includes in an upper 'flat' a small windowless room in which a stuccoed panel retains the matrix of a former wooden cross.[2] Beneath the cross is a low wooden cupboard with a step in front of it, as it were an altar or prayer-desk. Was this a little Christian oratory? It may have been. If so, it must have been there before A.D. 79 and holds a high priority in the archaeology of Christianity.

[1]See pages 146-149

[2]See page 143

Introduction

Jadis, comme aujourd'hui, la cité grecque de Néapolis ou Naples était orientée vers le sud et donnait sur un littoral en forme de courbe marqué par de petites villes reliées entre-elles par des fermes et maisons de campagne éparses. La vue est limitée par Capri, avec son sinistre mur de falaises et son empéreur Tibérius quasi légendaire; mais sous le paysage maintenant romain et moderne de la botte, il reste quelque chose de plus que le souvenir des colons helléniques qui furent les premiers à civiliser les Oscans natifs et à préparer la voie pour la domination romaine. L'urbanisme de Néapolis, tel que nous le connaissons, ainsi que ceux de Pompéi et d'Herculanum (la ville Héracleia ou Héracleion en grec), avec leurs blocs de bâtiments allongés ou *insulae*, ont leurs analogues dans des cités grecques telles que Olynthe. Ici se trouvent tous les éléments de la civilisation grecque, même si, en réalité, peu de ce qui est grec est apparent aujourd'hui. Les photographies assemblées dans ce livre nous montrent surtout les couches romaines datant des premiers siècles avant et après Jésus Christ.

Il est juste de dire, en parlant de Pompéi et d'Herculanum, que rien ne leur a tant réussi que d'abandonner leurs vies. Et par chance l'histoire de l'ensevelissement en l'an 79 après J. C. est inscrite dans la littérature par Pline le Jeune ayant assisté lui-même à l'événement et dont l'oncle le Naturaliste, un homme d'une curiosité et d'une érudition illimitées, périt en observant et relatant la conflagration puissante. Le neveu décrivit la scène peu de temps après dans une lettre célèbre adressée à son ami, l'historien Tacite.

Vers une heure de l'après-midi, le 24 août, la mère du narrateur attira l'attention de l'oncle de ce dernier sur un nuage qui assombrit soudainement les cieux de la Baie de Naples et dont on a constaté plus tard qu'il provenait du cratère du Vésuve. Il ressemblait, nous dit-on, au tronc d'un sapin élancé s'élargissant au faîte en un nombre de branches, un moment blanc, à un autre sombre et tacheté comme s'il transportait de la terre et des cendres. Pline l'Ancien, commandant d'une flotte près de Naples, fit manœuvrer ses galères et naviagua vers la scène du désastre afin d'observer de près le phénomène et de venir en aide, sans toutefois avoir une idée précise de la nature du besoin requis. Il débarqua à Stabies, au sud de Pompéi, se retira dans la maison d'un ami, prit son bain et «soupa plein d'une sérénité véritable ou affectée». Des pierres ponce et des cendres tombant troublèrent le sommeil de la maison; et le lendemain matin le vieux gentilhomme savant mais manifestement inefficace gisait asphyxié sur le rivage.

Depuis lors, les derniers jours de Pompéi furent élaborés par Lord Lytton et, par dessus tout, par des fouilles qui, depuis le 18ème siècle, ont mis à jour une partie considérable de la ville romaine et l'ont débarrassée de l'épaisse couche de lave et de cendres consolidées qui l'enterrait et la préservait tout à la fois dans une infinité de détails. Ici sur une table se trouvait le repas à moitié terminé consistant d'œufs, de poisson et de noix que les prêtres d'Isis avaient quitté précipitamment dans une vaine tentative de sauver les trésors de leur temple. Là dans un tombeau en dehors des enceintes de la ville une famille venait de célébrer le festin funèbre lorsque la porte du temple fut bloquée par de la lave et que les participants furent emprisonnés par la mort. Ailleurs, des cruches à vin et des timbales étaient prêtes dans la taverne, et de la menue monnaie se trouvait dans le tiroir-caisse. Un chien enchaîné, oublié dans la panique, avait péri dans sa lutte désespérée. Tout aussi oublié étaient deux prisonniers menottés et éten-

dus dans les communes des gladiateurs, près de l'amphithéâtre. Dans une autre pièce des communes, au milieu d'une foule de squelettes, se trouvait celui d'une femme ornée de bijoux magnifiques — et des potins archéologiques ont couru les rues. Ailleurs encore, le cadavre d'une femme étraignait un bébé, tandis que deux petites filles se cramponnaient à sa robe. Et cétéra. Ceux-ci et beaucoup d'autres pompéiens, ensevelis par des cendres brûlantes ou asphyxiés par des fumées furent préservés tels des enclaves dans la lave enveloppante et furent recréés avec une exactitude surprenante en versant du plâtre liquide dans des moules de fer trempé. Ces statues de plâtre ont rendu avec éclat la vie aux habitants, qu'ils soient esclaves ou hommes libres, de la cité condamnée.

Toutefois, il faut admettre que, excepté ces reliques macabres gardées aujourd'hui dans des musées, une certaine mélancholie existe dans ces lieux. Des rues, des magasins et des maisons, dont beaucoup sont encore utilisables, leur donnent un sentiment d'actualité et en même temps de vide sinistre que des hordes de touristes étrangers ne font qu'accentuer. Une vie réelle et pertinente a en effet cessé d'exister ici à une heure de l'après-midi de ce jour d'août.

Ce n'est qu'une seule fois lors de mes visites répétées que je me suis senti en harmonie avec cet abandon. Le soir du 30 septembre 1943, ma caravane militaire fut conduite à l'abri du porche de l'amphithéâtre aussi loin qu'un nouveau cratère fait par une bombe le permit. De temps à autre, l'éclair d'un canon ou le sifflement plaintif d'un obus rompait la nuit grandissante. Très au-dessus, dans l'obscurité, l'oeil enflammé du volcan — il fut actif durant cette année — brillait au-dessous du Chariot. Dans l'intimité de l'aube, je marchais pour peu de temps vers les nouvelles fouilles où, grâce à des techniques soigneusement mises au point, les maisons se dressaient une nouvelle fois de toute leur hauteur, bordant les rues romaines avec une vraisemblance surprenante dans le demi-jour. En effet, elles furent si convaincantes que, dû à une erreur compréhensible, elles venaient d'être bombardées et que l'atmosphère était encore empreinte de ces explosifs puissants. Le moment était parfait. Pour la durée d'un instant dans cette deuxième mort, la rue entière redevenait vivante . . .

Probablement, les signes les plus éloquents de «l'homme de la rue» à Pompéi sont les avis et griffonnages fortuits sur le plâtre des maisons. Ces graffites sont en effet presque l'image culturelle de la population. Des centaines de ceux-ci sont sous forme d'avis aux élections, quelques uns apparemment écrits par des amateurs, tandis que d'autres, de toute évidence, ont été peints par des gens habiles et de métier. En effet, un de ces hommes de métier faisait connaître son nom, et sa maison était commodément identifiée par ses clients par un avis peint à l'extérieur, indiquant «Aemilius Celer vit ici». Les avis peuvent se borner à décrire leur candidat comme «un homme bon»; toutefois, d'autres vont plus loin et déclarent qu'il est «un jeune homme digne de confiance», ou «un jeune homme d'une modestie incontestable». De l'un il est promis que «il sauvegardera soigneusement les finances de l'Etat». Une autre affiche dit «Proculus, fait Sabinus édile, et il ferait la même chose pour vous». Des afficheurs de l'opposition interviennent avec l'information que «les voleurs te demande de nommer Vatia édile» un autre affirme que «tous les soûlards et dormeurs» soutiennent le même infortuné Vatia. D'une manière plus charmante, Claudius est recommandé pour l'office de maire «par sa fiancée».

Ailleurs, les prochains spectacles de gladiateurs sont annoncés, et d'autres avis encore concernent des propriétés à vendre ou à louer; une des propriétés est décrite comme étant «désirable pour un chevalier».

Des gribouillages moins formelles comprennent, comme aujourd'hui, les noms des fainéants, quelquefois même avec des remarques ajoutées telles que «va et pendstoi». L'amour est naturellement un thème fréquent; résumé en un conseil, nous lisons: «nul n'est un gentilhomme qui n'a jamais aimé une femme». Le promeneur est également mis en garde de ce que «Restitutus a souvent déçu des filles». Mais, au milieu de tous ces persiflages surannées, il est intéressant de remarquer beaucoup de citations de poètes; Vergile, Ovide, Properce, Lucrète sont parmi ceux qui ont été identifiés. La connaissance littéraire universelle de l'homme de la rue à Pompéi est suffisamment évidente, et la mémorisation de la poésie est comprise comme une partie normale de son éducation.

Tandis que les murs de Pompéi sont couverts de slogans politiques, de personnalités et de grossièretés, il est probablement significatif que ceux d'Herculanum, 14 kilomètres plus haut sur la côte en direction de Naples, demeurent presque complètement insouillés, autant que nous puissions le savoir. Il y a d'autres évidences que Herculanum, moins d'un tiers de la grandeur de Pompéi, remplissait une fonction sociale différente et supérieure. Pompéi possédait des hommes d'une certaine aisance, mais était principalement une ville commerciale de classe moyenne. Herculanum avait également un peu de commerce mais — de toute façon jusqu'au séisme désastreux qui fit trembler toute la côte en l'an 63 après J. C. — cela était lié à une communauté prospère de personnes éduquées qui avaient choisi de vivre dans de confortables demeures à portiques, sur une colline soigneusement choisie en bordure de la mer, avec des terrasses et des belvédères appropriées à la sensibilité du siècle d'Auguste.

A l'encontre de Pompéi, qui fut enterrée sous les cendres et la lave, Herculanum fut noyée par un vaste torrent de boue volcanique. Ce flot de boue et ses conséquences sont le mieux observés par le visiteur dans les Bains des Faubourgs ou Bains de la Côte, un des édifices les plus récemment mis à jour.[1] C'est ici que la boue a préservé de façon intacte les portes de bois et autres objets que le choc a détachés. Il soit dit en passant que le bâtiment est également remarqué pour son architecture et pour la disposition des arches supportées directement par des colonnes qui ne fut guère en vogue que longtemps après durant la période romaine.

Des quatre blocs ou *insulae* découverts, l'un était consacré à l'usage des bains publics tels ceux qui formaient un rendez-vous populaire et sociale dans toutes les villes romaines. Quant au reste, chaque *insula* comprend soit une ou deux maisons de grandeur appréciable, souvent avec des peintures murales et des sculptures d'un intérêt considérable, et parfois avec un jardin en terrasses ayant ses prétensions. Au côte à côte de ces demeures de plus petites maisons existent, souvent associées aux magasins et aux ateliers dans un voisinage démocratique qui se trouve également à Pompéi mais qui, à Herculanum, représente plutôt une diminution du niveau de vie après le grand tremblement de terre. L'apparition des bâtiments élevés à plusieurs étages dans la banlieue indique une tendance similaire: l'affluence considérable du bas peuple dans la dernière phase de la ville et par conséquent la nécessité (pareille à ce qui se passe dans nos villes modernes) de construire des bâtiments plus élevés sur des terrains de plus en plus insuffisants et de valeur montant.

Une grande maison subdivisée en vue de loger un certain nombre de familles dans cette phase comprend dans un «appartement» supérieur une petite chambre sans fenêtres dans laquelle un panneau en stuc garde encore les empreintes d'une croix de bois antérieur.[2] Au-dessous de la croix se trouve une armoire basse faite de bois avec une marche devant, comme si c'était un autel ou un prie-dieu. S'agissait-il d'un petit oratoire? Cela aurait bien pu être. Si oui, il a dû se trouver ici avant l'an 79 après J. C. et tient un rang élevé dans l'archéologie de la chrétienté.

[1] Voir pages 146-149
[2] Voir page 143

Einleitung

Wer von Neapel, dem ursprünglich griechischen Neapolis, nach Süden blickt, gewahrt heute wie damals auf dem weiten Küstenbogen eine Reihe von Städtchen, zwischen denen zahllose Villen und Gehöfte das Landschaftsbild beleben. Den Abschluß der Aussicht bildet Capri mit seiner landseitig düsteren Steilküste und seinen legendären Erinnerungen an Kaiser Tiberius. Trotz ihrer römischen und modernen Prägung hat diese Landschaft im Kern etwas aus der Zeit der griechischen Kolonisation bewahrt, die der oskischen Urbevölkerung die ersten Grundlagen von Kultur vermittelte und so der späteren Römerherrschaft den Weg bereitete. Neapel sowohl wie Pompeji und Herculaneum (das griechische Herakleia oder Herakleion) mit ihren rechteckigen Wohnblocks oder *insulae* besitzen im Stadtplan eine unverkennbare Ähnlichkeit mit griechischen Städten wie Olynthos. Hier ist ein grundlegender Einfluß der griechischen Welt festzustellen. Im übrigen jedoch tritt heute nicht mehr viel Griechisches in Erscheinung. In den beiden ersten Jahrhunderten vor und nach Christi Geburt hat die römische Kultur völlig die Oberhand gewonnen. Die Abbildungen dieses Bandes sind ein sprechendes Zeugnis dafür.

Von Pompeji und Herculaneum kann man mit Recht sagen, daß kein Ereignis ihrer geschichtlichen Existenz die beiden Orte so berühmt gemacht hat wie ihr plötzlicher Untergang. Ein Augenzeugenbericht jener Katastrophe, die sich im Jahre 79 nach Christi ereignete, ist uns durch einen glücklichen Zufall erhalten. Er stammt von Plinius dem Jüngeren, dessen Onkel — als Naturforscher von unbegrenztem Erkenntnistrieb beseelt — das überwältigende Naturschauspiel eines Vulkanausbruchs aus nächster Nähe beobachten wollte und dabei ums Leben kam. Der Neffe schildert diesen tragischen Vorfall kurz danach in einem berühmten Brief an seinen Freund, den Geschichtsschreiber Tacitus.

Am vierundzwanzigsten August gegen ein Uhr mittags machte die Mutter des Briefschreibers den Onkel auf eine schwarze Wolke aufmerksam, die plötzlich den Himmel über der Bucht von Neapel verdunkelte und, wie sich später herausstellte, aus dem Krater des Vesuvs aufgestiegen war. Sie ähnelte — so wird uns berichtet — einer Pinie mit hohem Stamm, die sich oben zu einer Anzahl von Ästen verzweigte. Im ersten Augenblick weiß, wirkte sie im nächsten dunkel und wie gefleckt von erdigen und glühenden Bestandteilen. Plinius der Ältere, Befehlshaber einer Flotte in der Nähe von Neapel, stach alsbald mit seinen Galeeren in See und steuerte, um Näheres zu ergründen und zu helfen, auf die Stätte des Unheils zu, wahrscheinlich noch ohne klare Vorstellung von der Größe der Gefahr. Südlich von Pompeji, in Stabiae, ging er an Land, begab sich ins Haus eines Freundes, nahm ein Bad und „speiste mit wirklicher oder nur vorgegebener Heiterkeit". Die anschließende Nachtruhe der Hausinsassen wurde durch herabrieselnden Schlacken- und Aschenregen empfindlich gestört, und der folgende Morgen fand den gelehrten, aber in dieser Situation offenbar hilflosen alten Mann erstickt am Meeresufer vor.

Lord Lytton hat „Die letzten Tage von Pompeji" in seinem bekannten Roman ausführlich geschildert. Vor allem aber begannen seit dem 18. Jahrhundert die Ausgrabungen, und es gelang, einen beachtlichen Teil der alten Stadt von ihrer meterhohen Decke aus Lava und verfestigter Asche zu befreien, unter der sie nicht nur begraben, sondern bis in die kleinsten Details erhalten war. Hier stand noch die eben begonnene Mahlzeit von Eiern, Fisch und Nüssen auf dem Tisch, von dem die Isispriester überstürzt aufgestanden waren, um ihre Tempelschätze zu retten. Dort hatten sich in einem Mausoleum außerhalb der Stadtmauern die Familienmitglieder zu einer Begräbnisfeier versammelt und waren nun, eingeschlossen von den die Ausgangstür blockierenden Lavamassen, in gemeinsamem Tod vereint. Andernorts fand man Amphoren und Trinkbecher auf dem Schanktisch einer Taverne, und daneben lag in einem Kästchen das Wechselgeld. Ein in der Panik der Flucht vergessener Hund verendete hilflos an seiner Kette, und ebenso vergessen starben in der Gladiatorenkaserne beim Amphitheater zwei gefesselte Gefangene den Erstickungstod. In einer der Kasernenstuben fanden sich inmitten von Skeletten die Überreste einer reichgeschmückten Frau — ein Fund, der für die Mutmaßungen der Archäologen reiche Nahrung bot. An anderer Stelle wiederum hielt eine Frau ihren Säugling im Arm, während sich zwei kleine Mädchen an ihren Rock klammerten. Diese und viele andere Bewohner Pompejis, die durch den heißen Aschenregen zu Boden gestürzt waren oder durch die ausströmenden Gase erstickten, sind in ihrem Volumen in der sie umgebenden Lava konserviert, und durch Ausgießen solcher steinharter Höhlungen mit flüssigem Gips ließ sich ihre ehemalige Gestalt in geradezu erstaunlicher Vollständigkeit wiederherstellen. Mit einem beklemmenden Realismus erwecken diese Abgüsse die Einwohner der untergegangenen Stadt wieder zum Leben, freie Bürger und Sklaven in gleicher Weise.

Aber auch ohne diese makabren Relikte, die jetzt in Museen aufbewahrt werden, ist der Ort von einer seltsamen Melancholie erfüllt. Die freigelegten Straßen, Läden und Häuser, viele davon noch im Zustand des eben beginnenden Arbeitstags, wirken zugleich lebendig und trübselig öde, eine Atmosphäre, die durch die Scharen fremder Touristen noch zwielichtiger wird. Allein, die echte Realität des Daseins hat ein für allemal an jenem Augusttag des Jahres 79 mit dem Glockenschlag eins ihr jähes Ende gefunden.

Nur ein einziges Mal habe ich bei meinen zahlreichen Besuchen Pompejis diese Verlorenheit nicht empfunden. Am Abend des 30. September 1943 hatte ich mit meinem Armee-Caravan unter dem Eingang des Amphitheaters Deckung gesucht, wenigstens soweit ein frischer Bombenkrater dies zuließ. Dann und wann unterbrach ein Flintenschuß oder das eintönige Wimmern einer Granate die Stille der Nacht. Hoch oben im Dunkel, hinter dem Sternbild des Wagens, glühte das Flammenauge des Vesuvs, der in jenem Jahr gerade wieder in Tätigkeit war. Die ungestörte Stunde der Morgendämmerung benutzte ich zu einer Besichtigung der neuen Ausgrabungen. Dank einer sorgfältigen Grabungstechnik erhoben sich jetzt die Häuser wieder in voller Höhe und säumten im Schein des ungewissen Lichts die römische Straße erstaunlich lebensecht. Sie hatten sogar derart überzeugend gewirkt, daß man sie irrtümlich zum Ziel eines Bombenangriffs gewählt hatte, von dessen Brandgeruch die Luft noch getränkt war. Das Erlebnis der Stunde war einzigartig. Für einen kurzen Augenblick erweckte dieser zweite Tod die ganze Straße zu neuem Leben . . .

Die lebendigsten Spuren des pompejanischen Alltags sind uns in Aufschriften und Gelegenheitskritzeleien an den Hauswänden erhalten. Diese Sgraffiti stellen tatsächlich eine Art Querschnitt durch das kulturelle Leben Pompejis dar. Hunderte davon dienen der Wahlpropaganda. Manche sind primitiv hingemalt, andere stammen offensichtlich von der geübten Hand eines Fachmannes. Einer der Schreiber überliefert uns seinen Namen, indem er sein Haus für seine Kunden durch die Aufschrift kennzeichnet: „Hier wohnt Aemilius Celer". Manche Wahlempfehlungen begnügen sich damit, ihren Kandidaten als „einen guten Mann" zu bezeichnen. Andere gehen so weit zu behaupten, er sei „ein vertrauenswürdiger junger Mann" oder „ein junger Mann von unzweifelhafter Bescheidenheit". Von einem weiteren Kandidaten wird vielversprechend gesagt: „Er wird mit den öffentlichen Geldern sparsam umgehen". Eine Inschrift enthält die Aufforderung: „Proculus! Wähle Sabinus zum Aedilen, und er wird für dich dasselbe tun". Kämpferische Wahlpropa-

ganda versteigt sich zu der Behauptung, daß nur „Diebe dir raten, Vatia zum Aedilen zu wählen". Eine andere Notiz stellt fest, daß für besagten unglücklichen Vatia „alle Trunkenbolde und Herumtreiber" stimmen. Freundlicher klingt es, wenn Claudius von „seinem Liebhaber" für das Amt des Duumvirn empfohlen wird.

Weiterhin findet man Ankündigungen für Gladiatorenkämpfe oder Anzeigen über Verkauf und Verpachtung von Grundbesitz. Ein Anwesen wird „als würdig für einen vornehmen Herrn" bezeichnet. Ohne besondere Sorgfalt sind die Namen von stadtbekannten Taugenichtsen auf die Hauswände geschrieben, oft mit einem Zusatz wie zum Beispiel „geh und häng dich auf!" Die Liebe ist natürlich ein beliebtes Thema. Einmal faßt ein Vielerfahrener seine Weisheit in die Worte: „Keiner ist ein feiner Mann, der nicht ein Weib geliebt hat". Den Passanten wird auch nicht vorenthalten, daß „Restitutus oft und gern die Mädchen betrogen hat". Aber zwischen solchen Persiflagen finden sich interessanterweise auch viele Dichterzitate: Verse von Vergil, Ovid, Properz und Lucrez ließen sich identifizieren. Der durchschnittliche Pompejaner besaß offenbar eine gute Allgemeinbildung, und das Auswendiglernen von Gedichten bildete einen wichtigen Bestandteil seiner Erziehung.

Während die Wände Pompejis mit politischen Schlagzeilen, Namen und Neuigkeiten bedeckt sind, scheint dieser Brauch in Herculaneum, das doch nur fünfzehn Kilometer entfernt davon in Richtung Neapel lag, völlig unbekannt gewesen zu sein. Auch andere Erscheinungen deuten darauf hin, daß Herculaneum — kaum ein Drittel so groß wie Pompeji — einen ganz anderen Charakter besaß und auf einer höheren sozialen Stufe stand. In Pompeji gab es zwar viele wohlhabende Leute, aber es war nur eine Handelsstadt von mittlerem Niveau. Auch Herculaneum hatte seine geschäftliche Seite, allein diese spielte nicht die Hauptrolle, zumindest nicht vor dem Erdbeben vom Jahre 63, das alle Küstenorte heimsuchte: Hier lebten hauptsächlich reiche Familien von gehobener Bildungsstufe. Man besaß komfortable, mit einem Säulenportikus geschmückte Häuser, die auf einem besonders ausgewählten Hang mit dem Blick auf das Meer lagen, und nannte Terrassen und Aussichtstempel von augusteischem Geschmack sein eigen.

Anders als Pompeji, das unter einem Ge-

misch von Asche und Lava begraben lag, war Herculaneum von einem breiten Strom vulkanischen Schlamms überflutet worden. Die Auswirkungen dieses Schlammstroms kann man am besten an den Bädern vor der Stadt beobachten, die noch nicht lange freigelegt sind.[1] Hier haben sich sogar Holztüren und andere Ausstattungsstücke erhalten, wenn sie sich auch durch den Anprall der Schlammflut nicht mehr an ihrem alten Bestimmungsort befinden. Die Architektur dieser Bäder ist dadurch von besonderer Bedeutung, daß hier die Bogen unmittelbar auf den Pfeilern ruhen, eine Eigentümlichkeit, die sonst nur in spätrömischen Bauten anzutreffen ist.

Einer von den vier freigelegten Häuserblocks oder insulae der Innenstadt besitzt weitere öffentliche Bäder, die hier wie in allen römischen Städten den Treffpunkt des geselligen Lebens bildeten. Von den übrigen insulae enthält jede nur ein einziges oder höchstens zwei umfangreiche Wohnhäuser. Sie sind reich mit Wandgemälden und Skulpturen geschmückt und verfügen meist auch über einen anspruchsvoll ausgestatteten Terrassengarten. In anderen Stadtteilen stehen Wand an Wand mit solchen Patrizierhäusern kleinere Häuser, die oft auch mit Läden und Werkstätten versehen sind. Möglicherweise wurde diese Demokratisierung des städtischen Lebens sowohl in Pompeji als auch in Herculaneum durch den verminderten Lebensstandard nach dem großen Erdbeben bewirkt. Auf dieser Linie liegt auch der Bau von hohen Mietshäusern, wie sie am Rande der Stadt freigelegt wurden. In der letzten Phase der Stadt drängte offenbar die Masse der sozial niederen Landbewohner herein, und so ergab sich, genau wie in unseren modernen Städten, die Notwendigkeit wegen der ansteigenden Bodenpreise in die Höhe zu bauen.

Eines der hohen Häuser dieser späten Phase, das mehrfach unterteilt ist, um möglichst viele Familien aufnehmen zu können, enthält im obersten Stock einen kleinen fensterlosen Raum, in dem ein Stückpaneel Vertiefungen für ein Holzkreuz aufweist.[2] Unterhalb dieser Stelle befindet sich ein niedriger hölzerner Schrank mit einer Stufe davor, ein Aufbau, der an einen Altar denken läßt. Handelt es sich hier vielleicht um eine christliche Kapelle? Es erscheint nicht ausgeschlossen. Durch ihre Existenz vor dem Jahr 79 wäre sie eine der ältesten der Christenheit.

[1] Siehe Seiten 146-149
[2] Siehe Seite 143

Index Register

Pompeii
Pompéi
Pompeji

In A.D. 63 the cities of the Gulf of Naples were shaken by an earthquake which destroyed homes and public buildings. In Pompeii it burst the city reservoir and added floods to the havoc.

17 years later the citizens of Pompeii and Herculaneum were still rebuilding their damaged towns when they were overcome by a greater disaster. After centuries of quiescence the volcano of Vesuvius erupted. The sky became black as night, the air full of poisonous fumes, and a rain of red hot stones, volcanic ash and boiling mud descended over the surrounding countryside. The cataclysm lasted for three days; when it was over Pompeii was buried beneath stones and ashes, and Herculaneum covered by a sea of mud, in places 6o feet deep.

For four days before the eruption there had been earth tremors and many of the citizens, expecting another earthquake, may have left their homes — though how many really escaped and how many met their deaths in the countryside we cannot know. The people of Herculaneum had some chance to flee before the mud that came flowing down the mountain, but many citizens of Pompeii were struck down on the roads out of the city or overcome by poisonous fumes, while others, taking refuge in the cellars and inner rooms of their houses, were walled up by the volcanic debris and buried alive.

En l'an 63 ap.J.C., les cités du Golfe de Naples furent secouées par un tremblement de terre qui détruisit maisons et bâtiments publics. A Pompéi, le réservoir de la ville déborda et l'inondation fut ajoutée au tumulte.

17 ans plus tard les citoyens de Pompéi et de Herculanum étaient encore en train de reconstruire leurs villes endommagées lorsqu'un désastre encore plus cataclysmique déferla sur eux. Après plusieurs siècles de repos, Vésuve entra en éruption. Le ciel devint aussi noir que pendant la nuit, l'air se remplit de fumées empoisonnées et une pluie de pierres chauffées à blanc, de cendre volcanique et de boue bouillante descendit, enveloppant les pentes voisines. Ce cataclysme dura trois jours; après ces trois jours, Pompéi se trouva enseveli sous des pierres et de la cendre, et Herculanum était couvert d'une mer de boue, parfois ayant plus de 18 m de profondeur.

Il y avait eu, dans les quatre jours qui précédèrent l'éruption, des secousses de la terre et beaucoup de citoyens, craignant qu'il n'y eût encore des tremblements de terre, quit-

tèrent leurs maisons — mais nous ne pouvons jamais savoir combien en fait s'échappèrent et combien périrent dans les campagnes voisines. Les habitants d'Herculanum eurent quelque chance de fuir devant la boue qui envahissait la montagne, mais beaucoup de citoyens de Pompéi furent atteints sur les routes menant hors de la ville ou furent asphyxiés par les fumées empoisonnées, tandis que d'autres, ayant pris refuge dans les caves et chambres intérieures de leurs maisons, se trouvèrent emmurés par les débris volcaniques et ensevelis vivants.

Im Jahre 63 n.Chr. wurden die Städte im Golf von Neapel von einem schweren Erdbeben heimgesucht, das Heimstätten und öffentliche Gebäude zerstörte. In Pompeji barst das städtische Reservoir und fügte der Verheerung eine Überschwemmung hinzu.

17 Jahre später, die Bewohner von Pompeji und Herculaneum waren noch mit dem Wiederaufbau ihrer beschädigten Städte beschäftigt, wurden sie von einem noch größeren Unheil heimgesucht. Der Vesuv, ein während Jahrhunderten untätiger Vulkan, spie Feuer. Der Himmel wurde pechschwarz, die Luft verfinsterte sich mit giftigen Gasen und die umliegende Landschaft wurde von Bimssteinregen, vulkanischen Aschenlawinen und heißen Schlammströmen verwüstet. Der Vulkanausbruch dauerte drei Tage; nach diesen drei Tagen war Pompeji unter Steinen und Asche verschüttet und Herculaneum von einem Schlammeer überdeckt, teilweise bis zu 18 Metern Tiefe.

Vier Tage vor dem Ausbruch traten Erderschütterungen auf und viele der Bewohner, die ein anderes Erdbeben erwarteten, hatten ihre Heimstätten verlassen — doch werden wir nie wissen, wie viele entkommen konnten und wie viele den Tod auf dem Land fanden. Die Bevölkerung von Herculaneum hatte eine Chance, dem Schlamm, der sich in breiten Strömen den Berg hinunterwälzte, zu entfliehen, doch viele Bürger Pompejis wurden auf den stadtauswärts führenden Straßen zu Boden geschlagen oder von den Schwefeldämpfen erstickt, während andere, die in den Kellern und Innenräumen ihrer Häuser Zuflucht gesucht hatten, von den vulkanischen Gesteinsmassen eingemauert und lebendig begraben wurden.

Where people died in exposed places the lava
hardened around them to leave a hard mould.
By pouring liquid plaster into the cavity the
excavators have been able to preserve their
form.

Là où des gens moururent en plein air la lave
se durcit autour d'eux, laissant un moule dur.
En versant du plâtre liquide dans le creux, les
excavateurs ont pu préserver cette forme.

Wo Menschen an ungeschützten Orten starben,
erstarrte die sie umgebende Lava zu festem
Gestein und ließ eine harte Form zurück.
Indem die Gelehrten Gips in diese Höhlung
gossen, gewannen sie den Umriß eines Menschen, die Plastik eines toten Pompejaners.

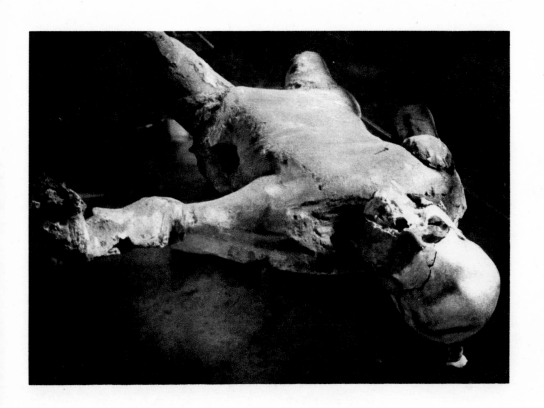

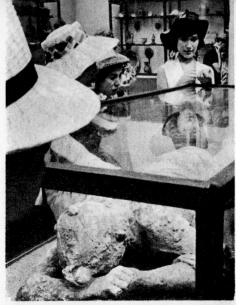

In the Pompeii Antiquarium modern tourists can see the fear and pain of that day nearly nineteen centuries ago in the attitudes of the dead.

Dans l'Antiquarium de Pompéi les touristes modernes peuvent voir la peur et la douleur de ce jour fatidique, il y a près de dix-neuf siècles, en regardant les poses des morts.

Im Antiquarium von Pompeji können die Touristen noch heute die Angst und den Schmerz jenes Tages, nach fast neunzehn Jahrhunderten sehen, die in den Stellungen der Toten ausgedrückt sind.

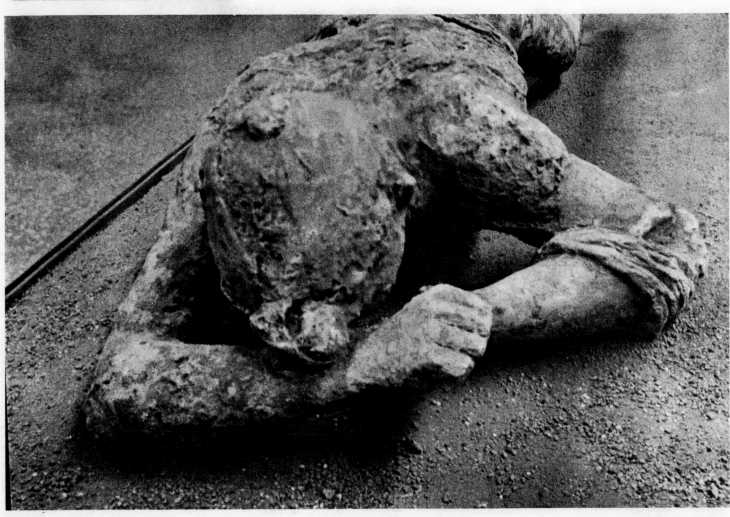

These people were overcome just outside the Porta Nuceria. Pompeii alone became a cemetary for 2,000 people.

Ces gens furent asphyxiés juste en dehors de la Porta Nuceria. Pompéi seul devint un cimetière pour 2.000 personnes.

Diese Menschen ereilte der Tod gerade vor der Porta Nuceria. Pompeji allein wurde ein Friedhof für 2.000 Menschen.

A muleteer, who tried to shelter against the wall of the portico of the Great Palaestra. He pulled his cloak up over his mouth to keep out the stifling vapours before they overcame him. His mule was found nearby.

Un muletier qui essaya de se protéger contre le mur du portique du Grand Palestre. Il tira sa cape sur sa bouche pour éviter de respirer les vapeurs suffocantes avant qu'elles ne l'asphyxièrent. On a retrouvé son mulet près de lui.

Ein Maultiertreiber, der sich schutzsuchend gegen die Mauer der Säulenhalle der Großen Palaestra gekauert hatte. Er zog seinen Umhang über seinen Mund, um die Schwefeldämpfe fernzuhalten, bevor sie ihn erstickten. Sein Maultier wurde in der Nähe gefunden.

Every beast of burden was used to speed the Pompeiians' flight and carry the belongings which they tried to take with them. Most of the animals found in the excavations were dogs. The one below, chained and forgotten in the House of Orpheus, died struggling to free himself; another, trapped with his master in the House of the Vestals, before dying of starvation, had eaten the man whose bones bear the dog's teethmarks.

Toutes les bêtes de somme furent utilisées pour faciliter la fuite hors de Pompéi en transportant des effets personnels. La plupart des animaux retrouvés dans les fouilles furent des chiens. Celui-ci, attaché et oublié dans la Maison d'Orphée, mourut en se débattant pour essayer de se libérer; un autre, pris avec son maître dans la Maison des Vestales, avait mangé l'homme avant de mourir de faim, comme le montre les marques de dents dans les os.

Alle Lasttiere wurden benutzt, um die Flucht der Pompejaner zu beschleunigen und die Habseligkeiten zu tragen, die jene mitzunehmen versuchten. Die meisten während der Ausgrabungen gefundenen Tiere waren Hunde. Dieser (Bild unten), der im Hause des Orpheus angekettet und dort vergessen wurde, starb, als er sich zu befreien versuchte; ein anderer, der mit seinem Meister im Hause der Vestalinnen eingeschlossen war, hatte den Menschen aufgefressen, bevor er dem Hungertod erlag, wie die Abdrücke der Zähne auf den Knochen zeigen.

A model of the Pompeii excavations in Naples Museum.

Un modèle des fouilles de Pompéi dans le Musée de Naples.

Ein Modell der Ausgrabungen in Pompeji, im Museum zu Neapel.

Pompeii was conquered by Rome in 290 B.C., though it was not until 89 B.C., following a rebellion put down by Sulla after a long siege, that Rome imposed her own way of life by installing veterans from her armies as colonists.

Pompeii's hot springs and the beauty of its situation in the Bay of Naples caused it to become a fashionable spa. Tiberius and Caligula built palaces at Sorrento and on the island of Capri. Along the shore and in the countryside surrounding the gulf more and more villas appeared. Factories and shops multiplied, commerce and industry flourished. As the city became more crowded and noisy many of the aristocrats took up residence in country villas outside the walls.

The city walls, with loopholes for archers and slingers to fire through, are from 25 to 33 feet high, according to the lie of the ground. An inner wall six feet higher prevented enemy projectiles from falling into the city. There were 12 watchtowers at the time of Sulla's siege in 89 B.C.; the walls still bear the marks made by his missiles. After Pompeii became a colony in 80 B.C. the name of Rome was considered sufficient protection and building began outside the walls.

Pompéi fut conquise par Rome en 290 av.J.C., mais ce ne fut qu'en 89 av.J.C., à la suite d'une rébellion supprimée par Sulla après un siège prolongé, que Rome imposa sa façon de vivre en installant des vétérans des armées comme colons.

Les sources d'eau chaude et la beauté du site même dans la Baie de Naples firent de Pompéi une ville d'eau à la mode. Tibérius et Caligula firent construire des palais à Sorrente et sur l'île de Capri. Sur la côte et dans la compagne voisine du Golfe, de nombreuses villas furent construites. Usines et magasins prospérèrent, le commerce et l'industrie se développa rapidement. Au fur et à mesure que la ville devint plus encombrée et bruyante, les aristocrates choisirent de vivre dans des villas bâties hors des murs.

Les murs de la cité, percés de trous pour permettre aux archers et aux frondeurs de tirer, ont de 7.5 à 10 mètres de haut, suivant la situation du sol. Un mur intérieur ayant près

de 2 m de plus empêcha les projectiles de l'ennemi de tomber dans la ville. En 89 av. J.C., il y avait, au moment du siège de Sulla, 12 tours de garde; les murs portent encore les marques faites par ces missiles. Une fois que Pompéi devint colonie en 80 av.J.C., le nom de Rome fut considéré protection suffisante et la construction commença en dehors du murs.

Pompeji wurde im Jahre 290 v.Chr. von Rom erobert, doch erst im Jahre 89 v.Chr., nachdem Sulla, nach einer langen Belagerung der Stadt, einen Aufstand derselben unterdrückt hatte, gelang es Rom, dieser Stadt ihre eigenen Lebensformen aufzuerlegen, indem Veteranen aus ihren Armeen als Kolonisten in Pompeji angesiedelt wurden.

Pompeji wurde aufgrund seiner heißen Quellen und der Schönheit seiner Lage in der Bucht von Neapel zu einem beliebten Badeort. Tiberius und Caligula erbauten Paläste in Sorrento und auf der Insel Capri. Dem Meeresufer entlang und in den die Bucht einsäumenden Gegenden schossen immer mehr Villen aus dem Boden. Fabriken und Geschäfte vermehrten sich, Handel und Industrie blühte. Als sich die Stadt immer stärker bevölkerte und immer lärmiger wurde, schlugen viele Aristokraten ihren Wohnsitz in Landvillen außerhalb der Stadtmauern auf.

Die Stadtmauern, mit Öffnungen für die Bogen- und Wurfschützen, sind zwischen 7,5 und 10 Meter hoch, je nach der Bodenlage. Eine 2 Meter höhere Innenmauer hielt feind-

liche Geschosse ab. Zur Zeit von Sullas Belagerung im Jahre 89 v.Chr. gab es 12 Wachttürme; die Mauern tragen noch heute die Spuren dieser Wurfgeschosse. Nachdem Pompeji im Jahre 80 v.Chr. römische Provinz wurde, galt der Name Rom als genügender Schutz und eine ausgedehnte Bautätigkeit begann außerhalb der Mauern.

The Porta Nola. In the centre of the arch is
a helmeted head of Minerva.

La Porta Nola. Au centre de l'arche, une
tête casquée de Minerve.

Die Porta Nola. In der Mitte des Bogens
ein behelmter Kopf der Minerva.

The Via Stabia, the main road for traffic to
the neighbouring port and towns on the Sorrentine coast. Note the stepping stones for
crossing the road

La Via Stabia, route principale pour la
circulation allant vers le port et les villes
voisines sur la côte sorrentine. Observez les
pierres de gué pour traverser la route.

Die Via Stabia, die Hauptverkehrsstraße zum
benachbarten Hafen und den Städten an der
Sorrentinischen Küste. Beachten Sie die Trittsteine zum Überqueren der Straße.

The Porta Nuceria. The city has eight gates; this one, built before Roman times, shows signs of later restoration and renovation.

La Porta Nuceria. La cité a huit portes celle-ci, construite avant l'époque romaine, porte des traces d'une restoration et d'une rénovation ultérieures.

Die Porta Nuceria. Die Stadt besitzt ach Tore; diese in vorrömischen Zeiten erbaute Pforte zeigt Spuren späterer Restaurierunger und Renovation.

The Forum, from the south. The centre of religious, political and economic life, as in every Roman city, the Forum was 480 feet long, 108 feet wide, and surrounded on three sides by a two-storeyed portico. To the south (foreground) the portico is a Samnite structure built in tufa, to the east and west Roman work in limestone which was still under construction at the time of the eruption. The columns would have been painted in vivid colour.

Le Forum, vu du Sud. Centre de la vie économique, politique et religieuse, comme dans toute ville romaine, le Forum avait 146 m de long et 32 m de large, entouré sur trois côtés par un portique à deux étages. Au Sud (avant-plan), le portique est une structure Samnite construite en tuffeau, à l'est et à l'ouest l'oeuvre romaine en calcaire qui était encore en cours de construction au moment de l'éruption. Les colonnes auraient été peintes en couleurs vives.

Das Forum, von Süden gesehen. Das Forum, Mittelpunkt des religiösen, politischen und wirtschaftlichen Lebens wie in jeder römischen Stadt, war 146 Meter lang, 32 Meter breit und auf drei Seiten von einem doppelgeschossigen Portikus umschlossen. Im Süden (Vordergrund) ist der Portikus eine samnitische Struktur aus Tuffstein, im Osten und Westen ein römisches Werk aus Kalkstein, das zur Zeit des Vesuvausbruchs noch im Bau war. Die Säulen wären in lebhaften Farben bemalt worden.

Left: At the north end of the Forum is the city's major temple, the Temple of Jupiter. In the distance beyond are the ominous peaks of Vesuvius.

A gauche: Au côté nord du Forum se trouve le temple principal de la ville: le Temple de Jupiter. Au fond les pics manaçants du Vésuve.

Links: Auf der nördlichen Schmalseite des Forums befindet sich der wichtigste Tempel der Stadt, der Jupitertempel. In der Ferne erblickt man die verhängnisvollen Spitzen des Vesuvs.

Right and left below: Brick columns of the Basilica, a building which served as both court and exchange, built late in the second century B.C.

A droite et à gauche en dessous: Les colonnes de la Basilique en briques, bâtiment qui servait à la fois de Cour de Justice et de Bourse, construite à la fin du deuxième siècle av. J.C.

Rechts und links unten: Kannelierte Backsteinsäulen der Basilika, ein Gebäude für Rechtspflege, Verkehr und Handel, das spät in dem zweiten Jahrhundert v. Chr. erbaut wurde.

Right: The western portico of the Forum. The many pedestals in the Forum once carried fine statues. The largest of these bases was probably the suggestum from which public orations were made.

A droite: Le portique ouest du Forum. Les nombreux socles dans le Forum supportaient jadis de belles statues. Le plus important de ceux-ci était probablement le *suggestum* d'ou se faisaient les discours publics.

Rechts: Der westliche Portikus des Forums. Die zahlreichen Piedestale im Forum trugen ehemals schöne Statuen. Der breiteste dieser Sockel war wahrscheinlich das *Suggestum*, von dem öffentliche Reden gehalten wurden.

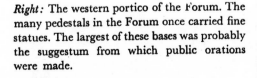

The Forum, from the north, seen through the Arch of Germanicus. Beyond, the east side of the Forum consists of the Macellum, a covered market with a fine portico of marble columns, the Temple of the Lares, the Temple of Vespasian, the headquarters of the Corporation of Fullers, and the Comitium, used for formalities connected with elections or with the courts.

Le Forum, vu du Nord, à travers l'Arche de Germanicus. Au loin, le côté est du Forum formé du *macellum*, marché couvert ayant un beau portique avec colonnes en marbre, le Temple des Lares, le Temple de Vespasien, le quartier général de la Corporation des Fouleurs et le *Comitium*, servant pour les formalités ayant trait aux élections ou à la justice.

Das Forum, vom Norden durch den Triumphbogen des Germanicus gesehen. Dahinter die östliche Längsseite des Forums mit dem *Macellum*, einer Markthalle mit schönem Portikus aus Marmorsäulen, dem Tempel der Laren, dem Tempel des Vespasian, dem Zunfthaus der Walker und dem *Comitium*, das bei Wahlen oder Gerichtsverhandlungen als Versammlungsraum diente.

The Temple of Jupiter in the Forum, seen from the Macellum. Seriously damaged in the earthquake of A.D. 63 it was still being rebuilt at the time of the eruption. The statue of Jupiter was stored in a crypt, awaiting installation in the reconstructed cella.

Le Temple de Jupiter et le Forum, vue du Macellum. Sérieusement endommagé lors du tremblement de terre de 63 après J.C., il était encore en cours de reconstruction lors de l'éruption. La statue de Jupiter fut placée dans une crypte, attendant son installation sur le socle reconstruit.

Der Jupitertempel und das Forum, vom *Macellum* aus gesehen. Durch das Erdbeben im Jahre 63 n.Chr. schwer beschädigt, befand er sich zur Zeit des Ausbruchs noch im Wiederaufbau. Die Statue des Jupiter wurde in einer Krypta aufbewahrt, bis sie in der wiedererstellten Cella aufgestellt werden sollte.

The Temple of Apollo, with Apollo represented as an archer, beside the Forum. The great court had a portico of 50 columns.

Le Temple d'Apollon, avec Apollon représenté comme un archer, près du Forum. La grande cour avait un portique de 50 colonnes.

Der Apollotempel, mit einem Standbild Apollos als Bogenschütze, neben dem Forum. Der große Platz war von einem Portikus aus 50 Säulen eingefaßt.

The temple contained altars to other gods, including Apollo's sister Diana, also represented as an archer (the original of her head is in Naples Museum).

Le temple contenait des autels pour d'autres dieux, dont Diane, soeur d'Apollon, représentée aussi comme archer (l'original de ce buste est au Musée de Naples).

Der Tempel enthielt Altäre für andere Gottheiten, darunter einen für Apollos Schwester Diana, die ebenfalls als Bogenschütze dargestellt wurde (das Original dieser Büste befindet sich im Museum zu Neapel).

Columns in the Temple of Apollo, with an inscription recording the names of the duumviri Sepanius and Herrenius, who erected a sundial here on the top of a column.

Colonnes du Temple d'Apollon, avec une inscription portant les noms des duumviri Sepanius et Herrenius qui firent placer ici un cadran solaire au sommet de la colonne.

Säulen im Apollotempel, mit einer Inschrift, die die Namen der Duumviri Sepanius und Herrenius überliefert, welche hier eine Sonnenuhr auf einer Kolonne errichten ließen.

Pompeii was also the home of exotic cults. These two pictures are of the Temple of Isis, whose worship was brought from Egypt and encouraged by Caesar's liaison with Cleopatra. The priests of the temple tried to save its treasure, flinging it into a sack before they fled. The priest carrying the sack fell first; the others picked him up, but several were killed by the collapse of a portico of the Triangular Forum nearby. The survivors took refuge in a house where they were finally trapped. One tried to cut his way out with a hatchet and broke through several walls but then died, still on his feet, the axe in his hand.

Pompéi était aussi le foyer de cultes exotiques. Ces deux photos montrent le Temple d'Isis;

la liaison de César et de Cléopatre avait encouragé cette adoration venue d'Egypte.
Les prêtres du temple essayèrent de sauver leurs trésors, les jetant dans un sac avant de fuir. Le prêtre portant le sac tomba le premier; les autres le soulevèrent, mais plusieurs furent tués lorsqu'un portique du Forum triangulaire voisin s'effondra. Les survivants se réfugièrent dans une maison où ils furent finalement pris. L'un des prêtres essaya de se frayer un chemin avec une hache et traversa plusieurs murs avant de mourir, encore debout, la hache dans la main.

Pompeji war auch das Zentrum exotischer Kulte. Diese zwei Bilder zeigen Ausschnitte aus dem Tempel der Isis, deren Verehrung von

Ägypten übernommen und durch Caesars Liaison mit Cleopatra gefördert wurde.
Die Priester versuchten, den Tempelschatz zu retten. Sie rafften die wertvollsten Stücke zusammen und verstauten sie vor ihrer Flucht in einen Leinensack. Der Priester, der den Sack trug, fiel als erster; die andern wollten ihn aufrichten, doch mehrere wurden dabei von einem niederstürzenden Portikus des nahegelegenen Forum triangulare getötet. Die Überlebenden suchten in einem Hause Schutz, wo sie schließlich eingeschlossen wurden. Einer versuchte, sich mit einer Axt einen Ausweg zu schlagen, er durchbrach mehrere Mauern, doch dann starb auch er, noch immer auf den Füßen, die Axt in der Hand.

After the Forum, the most important meeting place was the Thermae, the public baths. Here were not only turkish baths with warm rooms, hot rooms, cold plunges and masseurs, but a palaestra for sports and exercises, and probably a library. Pompeii may have been ahead of Rome in having a palaestra as part of her baths. Decorations, despite the steamy atmosphere, were sumptuous; even the lavatories, where Pompeiians liked to sit and chat, had marble seats and ornately carved armrests. *Above:* The calidarium (hot room) of the Forum Thermae.

Après le Forum, le lieu de réunion le plus important était les Thermes, ou bains publics. Ici il y avait non seulement des bains turcs avec des chambres tièdes, des chambres chaudes, des piscines d'eau froide et des masseurs, mais un palestre pour les sports et les exercices et probablement une bibliothèque. Pompéi était probablement en avance même sur Rome en ayant un palestre formant un tout avec les bains. Les décorations, en dépit de la vapeur de l'atmosphère, étaient luxueuses; même les cabinets de toilette, où les Pompéiens aimaient s'asseoir et bavarder, avaient des sièges en marbre et des accoudoirs sculptés avec art.
Ci-dessus: Le *caldarium* des Thermes au Forum.

Der wichtigste Versammlungsort neben dem Forum waren die Thermen, die öffentlichen Bäder. Hier gab es nicht nur türkische Bäder mit Masseuren, Räumen für Warm- und Heißluftbäder sowie Kaltwasserbecken, sondern auch eine Palaestra für jene Gymnastik, welche als Vorbereitung zum Baden diente, und wahrscheinlich eine Bibliothek. Pompeji war Rom vermutlich einen Schritt voraus, da eine Palaestra zu ihren Badeanlagen gehörte. Die Thermen waren, trotz der dampfdurchschwängerten Luft, prunkvoll ausgestattet; sogar die Waschräume, in denen die Pompejaner sich gern aufhielten und plauderten, hatten Marmorsitze und kunstvoll gemeißelte Armstützen.
Oben: Das *Caldarium* (warmes Wasserbad) der Forumthermen.

Atlantes support the ceiling in the tepidarium (warm room) of the Forum Thermae.

Les Atlantes soutiennent le plafond du *tepidarium* des Thermes au Forum.

Atlanten, die die Decke des Tepidariums (warmes Luftbad) in den Forumthermen tragen.

Entertainments played an important part in Pompeiian life. Performances in the theatre and the Great Amphitheatre were free, being paid for by civic dignitaries or those aspiring to office who wished to gain popularity. The Great Theatre can be seen on the left and the Odeon on the right. In the foreground is the quadroporticus, a large piazza which formed the foyer for the theatres and was later converted into a gladiatorial barracks.

Les spectacles constituaient une parte importante de la vie de Pompéi. Les représentations au théâtre et dans le Grand Amphithéâtre étaient gratuites, étant subventionnées par les dignitaires civils ou ceux qui cherchaient à gagner en popularité. Le Grand Théâtre peut être vu à gauche, l'Odéon à droite. A l'avant-plan est le *quadroporticus*, vaste piazza formant le foyer des théâtres et qui plus tard fut transformé en caserne pour les gladiateurs.

Volksbelustigungen spielten eine bedeutende Rolle im Leben Pompejis. Den Aufführungen im Theater und dem Großen Amphitheater konnte kostenlos beigewohnt werden, da sie von den öffentlichen Würdenträgern finanziert wurden oder von solchen Personen, die nach einem Amt trachteten und Popularität zu gewinnen hofften. Das Große Theater ist links, das Odeon rechts. Im Vordergrund befindet sich der Quadroporticus, eine breite Piazza, die das Foyer für die Theater bildete, und später in Gladiatorenkasernen umgewandelt wurde.

The Great Theatre, originally built between 200 and 150 B.C. in the Greek style, made use of a natural cavity in the hillside. Later enlarged by a Roman architect, Marcus Artorius Primus, it could probably seat as many as 5,000. The plays ranged from Greek tragedy to atellana. These farces, ancestors of the commedia dell'arte, were originally presented to relax the audience after some harrowing tragedy but were later played in their own right. The theatre was equipped with awnings (vela) to give shade on hot days, and a device for sprinkling the spectators with scented water. The stage, bigger than usual for a provincial theatre, was equipped with all the usual mechanism for scene changes and effects, and could be flooded for sea scenes. The curtain was lowered into a slot, not raised into the air.

Le Grand Théâtre, construit d'abord entre 200 et 150 av. J.C., dans le style grec, utilisait un creux naturel dans la colline. Agrandi plus tard par l'architecte romain Marcus Artorius Primus, il pouvait probablement contenir jusqu'à 5.000 spectateurs. Les pièces allaient des tragédies grecques aux atellanae. Ces farces, précurseurs de la commedia dell'arte, furent présentées à l'origine pour que les spectateurs puissent se détendre après une tragédie angoissante, mais elles furent jouées par la suite pour elles-mêmes. Le théâtre était équipé de *vela* (toiles) pour abriter du soleil et il y avait un dispositif pour humecter les spectateurs d'eau parfumée. La scène, plus grande que dans la plupart des théâtres de province, avait tous les mécanismes habituels pour changements de décor et effets, et pouvait être inondée pour scènes marines. Le rideau était abaissé par une fente, et non pas soulevé en l'air.

Das Große Theater, ursprünglich zwischen 200 und 150 v.Chr. im griechischen Stil erbaut, folgte einer natürlichen Senkung im Hügelabhang. Es wurde später vom römischen Architekten Marcus Artorius Primus vergrößert und konnte wahrscheinlich bis zu 5.000 Personen fassen. Die Stücke reichten von der griechischen Tragödie zur Fabula Atellana. Diese Schwänke, Vorläufer der Commedia dell'arte, wurden ursprünglich aufgeführt, um die Zuschauer nach einer ernsten Tragödie zu entspannen, doch später bekamen sie eine selbständige Theatergattung. Das Theater konnte durch ein Zeltdach (vela) überdeckt werden, das an heißen Tagen Schatten spendete; es besaß auch eine Vorrichtung zum Besprengen der Zuschauer mit parfümiertem Wasser. Die Bühne, größer als in den meisten Provinztheatern, war mit all den gebräuchlichen Mechanismen für Szenenwechsel und Bühnenwirkungen ausgestattet und konnte für Meeresszenen überflutet werden. Der Vorhang wurde in eine Vertiefung gesenkt, und nicht in die Luft gehoben.

Left: The Odeon was built between 80 and 75 B.C. at the expense of two wealthy magistrates, M. Porcius and C. Quinctius Valgus. It could hold between 1,000 and 2,000 spectators, and attracted a more select audience than the Great Theatre. It was used more for musical and mime performances and recitals. Productions were much less elaborate than those in the big theatre.

A gauche: L'Odéon fut construit entre 80 et 75 av. J.C. aux frais de deux magistrats riches, M. Porcius et C. Quinctius Valgus. Il y avait place pour 1000 à 2000 spectateurs, et il attirait un auditoire plus raffiné qu'au Grand Théâtre. Ce théâtre donnait surtout des représentations musicales et de mime ainsi que des concerts. Les mises en scène étaient moins compliquées qu'au Grand Théâtre.

Links: Das Odeon wurde in den Jahren 80—75 v.Chr. auf Kosten zweier reicher Magistraten, M. Porcius und C. Quinctius Valgus, erbaut. Es konnte zwischen 1.000 bis 2.000 Zuschauer fassen und zog ein verfeinerteres Publikum an als das Große Theater. Hier wurden vor allem musikalische Aufführungen, Gebärdenspiele und Konzerte gegeben. Die Darbietungen waren viel rudimentärer als jene des Großen Theaters.

The auditorium of the Odeon, showing the carved tufa Telamones at the end of the side parapet (right) and the griffon which marks the end of the division between the seating for the general public and that for dignitaries (above). Although the theatre was built in Roman times these decorations recall the style of Hellenic theatres.

La salle de l'Odéon, montrant les cariatides sculptés au bout du parapet latéral (à droite) et le griffon qui indique le partage entre les fauteuils pour le public en général et pour les dignitaires (dessus). Bien que le théâtre fut construit à l'époque romaine, ces motifs rappellent le style des théâtres helléniques.

Das Auditorium des Odeons, mit den aus Tuffstein gemeißelten Karyatiden am Ende der Seitenbrüstung (rechts) sowie dem Greifen, der das Ende der Aufteilung zwischen den Plätzen für das allgemeine Publikum und jenen für die Würdenträger bezeichnet (oben). Obwohl das Theater in römischer Zeit erbaut wurde, erinnern diese Ausschmückungen an den Stil hellenischer Theater.

The Great Amphitheatre, 142 yards at its widest point, was big enough to hold 20,000 spectators — probably as many as the entire population of Pompeii. The oldest known Roman amphitheatre, it was built about 80 B.C., largely at the expense of the two magistrates who built the Odeon. The upper galleries, which were probably reserved for women, are reached by external stairs.

Le Grand Amphithéâtre, ayant jusqu'à 130 m de large, pouvait contenir 20.000 spectateurs — vraisemblablement toute la population de Pompéi. Le plus ancien des amphithéâtres romains, celui-ci fut construit vers 80 av. J. C., surtout aux frais des deux magistrats qui construisirent l'Odéon. Les galeries supérieures, probablement réservées pour les femmes, sont atteintes par des escaliers extérieurs.

Das Große Amphitheater, mit einem größten Durchmesser von 130 Metern, konnte 20.000 Zuschauer fassen — wahrscheinlich so viele wie die gesamte Bevölkerung von Pompeji. Es ist das älteste römische Amphitheater, das wir kennen, und wurde um die Jahre 80 v.Chr. erbaut. Die Kosten wurden größtenteils von den beiden Magistraten bestritten, die das Odeon erbaut hatten. Die oberen Galerien, die wahrscheinlich für Frauen reserviert waren, werden durch eine äußere Treppe erreicht.

The arena and seats of the Amphitheatre, where the savage spectacles of animals and gladiators fighting to the death were the favourite entertainment of the bloodthirsty populace. Unlike the larger amphitheatres of the Imperial period there are no subterranean passages beneath the arena.

Feeling ran so high at one performance that a pitched battle broke out between Pompeiians and men in the audience from nearby Nuceria, and Nero banned performances at Pompeii for ten whole years (A.D. 59—69).

L'arène et les fauteuils de l'Amphithéâtre, où les spectacles d'animaux et de gladiateurs luttant à mort étaient la récréation préférée de la population sanguinaire. Contrairement aux amphithéâtres plus grandes construits sous l'Empire, il n'y a pas de passages souterrains sous l'arène.

A un spectacle l'émotion fut si vive qu'une bataille rangée éclata entre Pompéiens et habitants de Nuceria, ville voisine. Néron défendit toute représentation à Pompéi pendant dix longues années (59—69 après J. C.)

Die Arena und die Zuschauerplätze des Amphitheaters, wo die wilden Schauspiele der Tiere und Gladiatoren, die auf Leben und Tod miteinander kämpfen mußten, die bevorzugte Unterhaltung des blutdürstigen Pöbels waren. Im Gegensatz zu größeren Amphitheatern der Kaiserzeit gibt es hier keine unterirdischen Gänge unter der Arena.

In einem Kampfspiel führte der leidenschaftliche Anteil der Zuseher zu einem äußerst erbitterten Kampf zwischen Bewohnern von Pompeji und solchen aus dem nahegelegenen Nuceria . . . woraufhin Nero Darbietungen in Pompeji für zehn lange Jahre (59—69 n. Chr.) untersagte.

View of the arena from the North entrance.

Vue de l'arène prise de l'entrée nord.

Sicht auf die Arena durch den Nordeingang.

A typical Pompeiian street. Note the raised
pavements and the stepping stones for crossing
the road. The cartwheel (from a cast in the
Antiquarium) is of the type which gouged ruts
in the paving stones.

Vue typique d'une rue à Pompéi. Notez les
trottoirs surélevés et les pierres de gué pour
traverser la rue. La roue de charrette (d'un
moulage dans l'Antiquarium) est du genre
qui creuse des rigoles dans les pavés

Eine typische Straße Pompejis. Beachten Sie
die erhöhten Trottoirs und die Trittsteine
zum Überqueren der Straße. Das Wagenrad
(nach einem Abguß im Antiquarium) ist
solcherart, daß es tiefe Räderspuren auf den
Pflastersteinen zurückläßt.

Fountain jets, from various public fountains. Pompeii had an excellent free water supply. Pressure was maintained by distribution centres. For those houses which did not have piped water, and for the hot and thirsty passers-by, there were public fountains at many street corners.

Jets de fontaines, de différentes fontaines publiques. Pompéi avait un excellent service d'eau gratuite. La pression était maintenue par des centres de distribution. Pour les maisons qui n'avaient pas d'eau courante, et pour les passants assoiffés et ayant chaud, il y avait des fontaines publiques à de nombreux coins de rue.

Strahlrohre, von verschiedenen öffentlichen Brunnen. Pompeji besaß eine ausgezeichnete unentgeltliche Wasserversorgung. Der Druck wurde mittels Verteilerzentren erhalten. Für jene Häuser, die keine Wasserleitungen besaßen sowie für die erhitzten und durstigen Spaziergänger gab es öffentliche Brunnen an vielen Straßenecken.

Left: The premises of Verecundus, a clothier, on the Via dell'Abbondanza, a popular shopping street. Only the frontage has been excavated; there were probably extensive workshops behind.

A gauche: Le local de Verecundus, un drapier, sur la Via dell'Abbondanza, rue commerçante. L'avant seulement a été fouillé; il y avait probablement des ateliers étendus derrière.

Links: Das Grundstück des Verecundus, eines Tuchmachers, auf der Via dell'Abbondanza, einer beliebten Einkaufsstraße. Nur die Vorderfront wurde ausgegraben; es gab wahrscheinlich ausgedehnte Arbeitsräume im hinteren Teil.

Right: On the right of Verecundus's door is this painting of the Venus of Pompeii, the city's special goddess. She wears a crown, carries a sceptre, and is riding in a quadriga drawn by four elephants. The technique is greatly superior to that of the painter of Mercury (opposite). In the panel below are shown the processes of Verecundus's trade: carding, dying, and a salesman (perhaps the owner himself) displaying the finished cloth.

A droite: Cette peinture de la Vénus de Pompéi, déesse attitrée de la ville, se trouve à droite de la porte de Verecundus. Elle porte une couronne et tient un sceptre à la main. Elle se trouve dans un attelage tiré par quatre éléphants. La technique de ce tableau est bien supérieure à celle du tableau représentant Mercure (en face). Dans le panneau inférieur on peut voir les procédés utilisés par Verecnndus: cardage, teinture; et un vendeur (peut-être le propriétaire lui-même) montrant le tissu fini.

Rechts: Zur rechten Seite der Tür des Verecundus-Hauses befindet sich diese Malerei der Venus von Pompeji, der Schutzgöttin der Stadt. Sie trägt eine Krone, hält ein Szepter und fährt in einer von vier Elefanten gezogenen Quadriga. Die Technik ist der vom Maler des Merkurs (gegenüber) angewandten überlegen. Auf der unteren Tafel wird der Arbeitsprozeß in Verecundus' Gewerbe gezeigt: Krempeln und Färben des Tuches und ein Verkäufer, (vielleicht der Besitzer selbst), der das fertige Tuch ausstellt.

A wall-painting on the left of the entrance to Verecundus's shop. It shows Mercury leaving a temple carrying a purse full of money. Perhaps Verecundus hoped this picture would stimulate the god to increase his prosperity. In the panel below a shopgirl is showing shoes to a young man.

Peinture sur un mur à gauche de l'entrée du magasin de Verecundus. On voit Mercure quittant un temple en portant une bourse pleine d'écus. Verecundus espérait peut-être que ce tableau inciterait le dieu à augmenter sa prospérité. Dans le panneau inférieur on voit une vendeuse montrant des souliers à un jeune homme.

Eine Wandmalerei auf der linken Seite des Eingangs zu Verecundus' Laden. Sie zeigt Merkur, der einen Tempel verläßt und einen gefüllten Geldbeutel trägt. Vielleicht hoffte Verecundus, daß dieses Bild den Gott ansporne, seinen Wohlstand zu vergrößern. Auf der untern Tafel zeigt ein Ladenmädchen einem jungen Mann Schuhe.

The Thermopolium of Assellinae, opposite Verecundus's shop. This was a bar serving hot and cold drinks. The names written on the walls suggest that the girls here were popular and perhaps very free with the customers.

Le Thermopolium d'Assellinae, en face du magasin de Verecundus. Ce cabaret vendait des boissons chaudes et froides. Les noms sur les murs indiquent que les filles étaient très populaires ici et peut-être cavalières avec les clients.

Das Thermopolium der Asellina, gegenüber Verecundus' Laden. Dies war ein Gasthaus, wo kalte und warme Getränke ausgeschenkt wurden. Die in die Wände eingeritzten

Namen weisen darauf hin, daß die Mädchen sehr beliebt waren und daß es dort auch noch andere Genüsse gab.

A bakery (pistrinum) in the Via di Stabia. In the foreground is the shop counter; behind are the flour mills. These consisted of two pieces of stone, the upper one being turned by a rod pushed through it. Grain was poured in at the centre of the top stone and ground between the two. (Of one mill only the conical lower stone remains.)

Une boulangerie (pistrinum) de la Via di Stabia. A l'avant-plan est le comptoir du magasin, derrière les minoteries. Ceux-ci consistaient en deux morceaux de pierre, le morceau supérieur tournant grâce à une barre qui le traverse. Le grain était versé au centre de la pierre supérieure et meulé entre les deux. (D'une des meules seulement la pierre conique inférieure reste).

Ein Backhaus (pistrinum) in der Via di Stabia. Im Vordergrund befindet sich der Ladentisch, dahinter die Mühlsteine. Diese bestanden aus zwei Steinen, wobei der obere mittels einer durch ihn getriebenen Stange gedreht wurde. Das Getreide wurde in der Mitte des oberen Steines eingeschüttet und zwischen den beiden Steinen zerrieben. (Von einer Mühle ist nur noch der kegelförmige untere Stein erhalten.)

The oven of another bakery.

Le four d'une autre boulangerie.

Der Ofen eines anderen Backhauses.

Above: a shop sign: 'Oil for sale'

Ci-dessus: Enseigne d'un magasin «Huile à vendre».

Oben: Das Schild eines Kaufladens: „Öl zu verkaufen".

Left: the counter of a shop (taberna) in the Via di Stabia, near the Odeon.

A gauche: Le compteur d'un magasin (taberna) dans la Via di Stabia, près de l'Odéon.

Links: Der Ladentisch eines Geschäftes (taberna) in der Via di Stabia, ganz in der Nähe des Odeons.

Right: a painting on the wall of a house attached to a bakery. It probably depicts the baker, Terentius, and his wife, but has also been identified as a portrait of the patrician P. Paquinas Proculus. He holds a book scroll and his wife a stylus and writing tablet. It is now in Naples Museum.

A droite: Peinture sur le mur d'une maison voisine de la boulangerie. Montre probablement Terentius, le boulanger, et sa femme, mais cette peinture a également été identifiée comme le portrait du patricien P. Paquinas Proculus. Il tient un rouleau de papier et sa femme un stylus et une tablette pour écrire. Dans le Musée de Naples.

Rechts: Eine Wandmalerei in einem mit dem Backhause verbundenen Haus. Sie stellt wahrscheinlich den Bäcker, Terentius, und seine Frau dar, doch wurde sie ebenfalls als ein Porträt des Patriziers P. Paquinas Proculus identifiziert. Er hält eine Pergamentrolle und seine Frau einen Schreibstift und ein Wachstäfelchen. Diese Malerei befindet sich jetzt im Museum zu Neapel.

Left: The street beside the central baths where it joins the Via di Nola. The phallus design on the left wall was a widespread symbol of good luck.

A gauche: La rue près des bains publics au carrefour de la Via di Nola. Le dessin d'un phallus sur le mur de gauche était un symbole de chance très commun.

Links: Die Straße neben den Zentralthermen, an der Kreuzung mit der Via di Nola. Die Phalluszeichnung auf der linken Mauer war ein sehr verbreitetes Glückssymbol.

The House of the Centenary in the Via di Nola. The peristyle had a two-storey colonnade.

La Maison du Centenaire dans la Via di Nola. Le péristyle a une colonnade sur deux étages.

Das Haus des Zentenars in der Via di Nola. Das Peristyl bestand aus einer zweigeschossigen Kolonnade.

The House of Paquius Proculus; this mosaic of animals and birds in panels leads through into the atrium.

La Maison de Paquius Proculus; cette mosaïque d'animaux et d'oiseaux en panneaux mène jusqu'à l'atrium.

Das Haus des Paquius Proculus; dieses Tier- und Vogelmosaik auf Tafeln führt bis ins Atrium.

Left: The entrance to the House of Quartio, near the Amphitheatre. The upper part of the bronze door is still in place.

A gauche: L'entrée de la Maison de Quartio, près de l'Amphithéâtre. La partie supérieure de la porte en bronze est encore en place.

Links: Der Eingang in das Haus des Quartio, nahe des Amphitheaters. Der Oberteil der Bronzetür befindet sich noch an Ort und Stelle.

Right: A mosaic in the entrance vestibule.

A droite: Mosaïque se trouvant dans le vestibule d'entrée.

Rechts: Ein Mosaik in der Eingangshalle.

Details showing Alexander and Darius from a mosaic of the Battle of Issus, which decorated the floor of the peristyle in the House of the Faun (now in Naples Museum).

Détails montrant Alexandre et Darius. Mosaïque de la bataille d'Issus, qui embellit le plancher du péristyle de la Maison du Faune (maintenant au Musée de Naples).

Darstellungen Alexanders und Darius, Ausschnitte aus einem Mosaik über die Schlacht von Issus, das den Fußboden des Peristyls im Hause des Fauns schmückte (nun im Museum zu Neapel).

The House of the Faun, one of the most beautiful examples of a private dwelling to have survived from ancient times. This was possibly the home of P. Sulla who was in charge of the reorganisation of the first Roman colony. Built at the peak of the Samnite period it shows considerable Hellenistic influence in plan and decoration.
In the centre of the coloured marble impluvium basin stood the statuette (original now in Naples Museum) from which the house takes its name.

La Maison du Faune, un des plus beaux exemples d'une maison particulière ayant survécue depuis l'antiquité. Probablement la maison de P. Sulla qui était responsable de la réorganisation de la première colonie romaine. Construite à l'apogée de la période samnite, on voit l'influence helléniste considérable dans le plan et la décoration.
Au centre du bassin en marbre de couleur de la cour intérieure se trouvait la statuette (l'original est maintenant dans le Musée de Naples) qui a donné son nom à la maison.

Das Haus des Fauns, eines der wunderbarsten Beispiele privater Wohnkultur, das aus der Antike noch erhalten ist. Dies war wahrscheinlich das Heim des P. Sulla, der für die Reorganisation der ersten römischen Kolonie verantwortlich war. Dieses in der Blütezeit der samnitischen Periode erbaute Haus zeigt in seiner Anordnung und Dekoration beträchtlichen hellenistischen Einfluß auf.
In der Mitte des aus farbigem Marmor erstellten Impluvium-Bassins erhob sich die Statuette (das Original ist nun im Museum zu Neapel), nach welcher das Haus benannt wird.

The kitchen and bathrooms of the House of the Faun, from its second, tetrastyle atrium. The passage at the far side of the peristyle leads through to a larger peristyle with a big garden.

Cuisine et salles de bain de la Maison du Faune du deuxième atrium tetrastyle. Le passage au fond du péristyle mène à un péristyle plus important avec un grand jardin.

Küche und Baderäume im Hause des Fauns, von seinem zweiten, viersäuligen Atrium aus gesehen. Der Gang an der entfernt liegenden Seite des Peristyls führt zu einem größeren Peristyl mit einem ausgedehnten Garten.

The portico of the bath in the Villa of Julia Felix. The owner, a business woman, let off some of the property as a shop, an inn, and small apartments with private entrances. She had also opened her baths to the public and advertised them as balneum venereum (baths fit for Venus).

Portique du bain dans la Villa de Julia Felix. La propriétaire, une femme d'affaires, souslouait une partie de la propriété comme magasin, auberge et petits appartements avec entrées particulières. Elle accueillait aussi le public aux bains qu'elle décrivait comme des *balneum venereum* (bains convenant à Vénus).

Portikus des Badehauses in der Villa der Julia Felix. Die Besitzerin, eine Geschäftsfrau, vermietete Teile dieses Anwesens als Laden, Gasthaus sowie kleine Wohnungen mit Separateingängen. Sie hatte auch ihre Bäder der Allgemeinheit zugänglich gemacht und pries sie als *balneum venereum* an (Bäder, geeignet für die Venus).

The porticoed garden, which has a fish-pond down the centre. The property was extensive enough, with its vegetable garden and orchard, to warrant calling it a villa, although it was within the city walls.

Jardin avec Portiques, ayant un étang pour poissons au milieu. La propriété était suffisamment importante, avec jardin potager et verger pour l'appeler une villa, bien qu'elle se trouve dans l'enceinte de la cité.

Der vom Portikus umfaßte Garten, in dessen Mitte sich ein Fischteich befindet. Das Besitztum war ausgedehnt genug, mit seinem Gemüse- und Obstgarten, um es eine Villa nennen zu können, obwohl es sich innerhalb der Stadtmauern befand.

Left: The atrium of the House of Menander.

A gauche: L'atrium de la Maison de Ménandre.

Links: Das Atrium des Hauses des Menander.

Right: A corridor leading to the peristyle of the House of Menander.

A droite: Couloir menant au péristyle de la Maison de Ménandre.

Rechts: Ein Gang, der zum Peristyl des Hauses des Menander führt.

Below: A shrine for the family cult in an alcove of the peristyle in the House of Menander. These casts reproduce the wax or wooden images as they had survived.

En dessous: Autel pour le culte de famille dans une alcôve du péristyle de la Maison de Ménandre. Ces moulages reproduisent les images en cire ou en bois telles qu'elles ont survécu.

Unten: Ein Altar für den Familienkult in einer Nische des Peristyls im Hause des Menander. Diese Abgüsse geben die Wachs- oder Holzfiguren so wieder, wie sie erhalten blieben.

The peristyle of the House of the Golden Cupids. The west end of the peristyle is raised *(left)* like a stage and many of the reliefs and hermae in the garden carry theatrical masks. The building was named after the decoration of one of the cubicles, cupids engraved on gold foil and placed under glass discs. The relief of Pan, and other reliefs set in the south wall of the portico, are further evidence of the owner's interest in the arts.

Le péristyle de la Maison des Cupidons Dorés. L'extrémité ouest du péristyle est surélevée *(à gauche)* comme une scène et beaucoup des reliefs et bustes du jardin portent des masques de théâtre. Le bâtiment tient son nom de l'ornement d'un des alcôves, des cupidons gravés sur feuille d'or et placés sous des disques en verre. Le relief de Pan et autres reliefs placés dans le mur sud du portique montrent que le propriétaire s'intéressait aux arts.

Das Peristyl des Hauses der Goldenen Cupidos. Das Westende des Peristyls ist wie eine Bühne gehoben *(links)* und viele der Reliefs und Hermen im Garten tragen Schauspielermasken. Das Gebäude erhielt seinen Namen nach der Dekoration einer Kammer, wo Goldfolien mit Cupidos graviert und unter Glasscheiben gelegt wurden. Das Relief des Pan, sowie andere in die Südmauer des Portikus gesetzte Reliefs geben Zeugnis von dem Kunstinteresse des Besitzers.

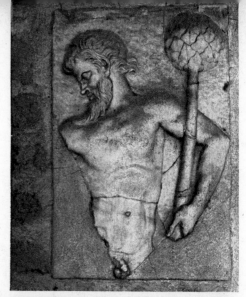

Right: The fountain in the House of the Great Fountain.

A droite: La fontaine dans la Maison de la Grande Fontaine.

Rechts: Der Springbrunnen, im Hause der Großen Fontäne.

Theatrical masks from the House of the Great Fountain. Placed in a niche, and decorated with brilliant glass paste mosaic, the fountain was a style imported from Graeco-Roman Egypt, particularly popular in post-Augustan times. The water flowed through the aperture below the central face and down the stepped facade.

Masques de théâtre de la Maison de la Grande Fontaine. Placée dans une niche, ornée de mosaïques colorées en verre, la fontaine était d'un style Gréco-Romain importé d'Egypte, à la mode surtout à l'époque post-Auguste. L'eau coulait par l'ouverture sous la face centrale et sur la façade étagée.

Schauspielermasken aus dem Hause der Großen Fontäne. Die in einer Nische erbaute Fontäne, mit glänzenden Glaspasten-Mosaiken verziert, war in einem von Ägypten eingeführten griechischrömischen Stil erstellt, der in nach-augusteischen Zeiten besonders beliebt war. Das Wasser ergoß sich aus der Öffnung unterhalb des mittleren Antlitzes und floß dann die stufenförmige Fassade hinunter.

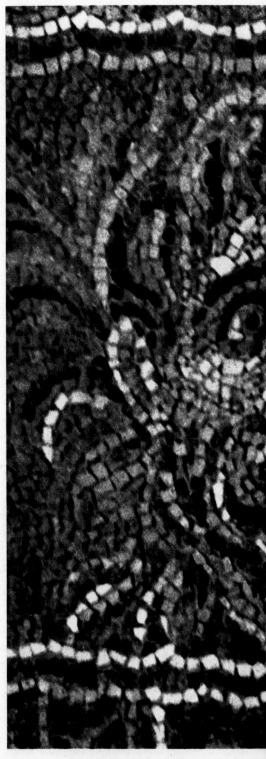

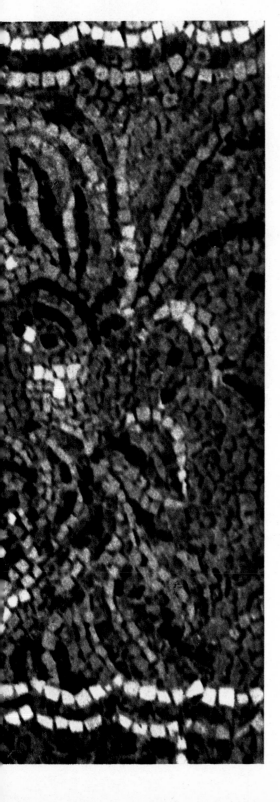

Left: The house of Cornelius Rufus. Two table-supports stand beside a marble impluvium, which caught the rainwater from a central skylight, but may in origin have been a hearth. Beyond is the peristyle.

A gauche: La maison de Cornelius Rufus. Deux supports sont placés à côté d'un bassin en marbre (impluvium) qui captaient l'eau de pluie d'une lucarne mais qui, à l'origine, était peut-être un foyer. Au fond le péristyle.

Links: Das Haus des Cornelius Rufus. Zwei Tischträger stehen neben einem marmornen Impluvium, das das Regenwasser von einem Dachfenster fing, das aber ursprünglich vielleicht ein Herd war. Dahinter das Peristyl.

The House of the Venus Marina, was being redecorated at the time of the eruption but the rich decorations of the garden had nearly reached completion. On one side of the garden *(right)* is painted a figure of Mars; on the other *(above)* a marble bowl on a pedestal with birds drinking. The lush painted foliage was designed as an integral part of the living garden.

La Maison de la Vénus Marina était en cours de réparation au moment de l'éruption mais les riches décorations du jardin avaient presque été terminées. D'un côté du jardin *(à droite)* Mars est représenté comme une statue peinte; de l'autre *(dessus)* un bol en marbre sur un piédestal avec des oiseaux qui boivent. Les flamboyants feuillages peints furent conçus somme faisant partie intégrale du jardin dans son ensemble.

Das Haus der Venus Marina wurde zur Zeit der Eruption neu dekoriert, doch die prachtvollen Ausschmückungen des Gartens waren beinahe vollendet. Auf der einen Seite des Gartens *(rechts)* steht ein bemaltes Standbild des Mars; auf der andern Seite *(oben)* befindet sich eine Marmorschale auf einem Sockel mit trinkenden Vögeln. Das in lebhaften Farben gemalte Laubwerk bildete einen integralen Teil des Gartens.

The atrium of the House of M. Lucretius
Fronto

L'atrium de la Maison de M. Lucretius Fronto.

Atrium des Hauses des M. Lucretius Fronto.

The peristyle of the House of Pansa surrounds
a pool instead of the usual garden.

Le péristyle de la Maison de Pansa entoure
une mare au lieu du jardin usuel.

Das Peristyl des Hauses des Pansa umgibt
einen kleinen Teich statt des herkömmlichen
Gartens.

'Beware of the Dog'. Mosaic pavement in the entrance of the House of the Tragic Poet.

«Prenez garde au chien». Mosaïque dans l'entrée de la Maison du Poète Tragique.

„Hüte dich vor dem Hund". Mosaikfußboden in der Eingangshalle des Hauses des Tragischen Poeten.

Left: A view from the entrance of the House of the Tragic Poet, across the atrium to the peristyle, with its lararium or household shrine in the form of a small temple. The building was named after a theatrical mosaic found here, now in Naples Museum.

A gauche: Vue de l'entrée de la Maison du Poète Tragique, avec ensemble de l'atrium et du péristyle avec le *lararium* ou sanctuaire familial sous forme de temple. Le bâtiment tient son nom d'une mosaïque théâtrale qui y fut trouvée, maintenant dans le Musée de Naples.

Links: Der Eingang des Hauses des Tragischen Poeten, mit Durchblick auf das Atrium und das Peristyl mit seinem *Lararium* oder häuslichen Schrein in der Form eines kleinen Tempels. Das Gebäude wurde nach einem hier gefundenen Theater-Mosaik benannt, das sich nun im Museum zu Neapel befindet.

The Pompeiians delighted not only in painting their walls, but in adorning their homes with statuary of marble and bronze. They set such value upon it that they took as much as possible with them when they escaped, and many afterwards returned to the buried city to salvage what they could. One wealthy merchant, Publius Cornelius Teges, had a fine copy of a famous Greek figure of an ephebus, a Greek youth under military training, adapted as a lampstand, with a lamp held in the right hand. He dismantled it, and was carrying it away when he was overwhelmed and buried under the ceiling of his own home, known today as the House of the Ephebus.

Non seulement les Pompéiens adoraient peindre leurs murs, mais ils aimaient aussi remplir leurs maisons de statues en marbre et en bronze. Ils attachaient tant de valeur à ces statues qu'ils essayèrent de les emmener avec eux dans leur fuite, et beaucoup retournèrent plus tard dans la ville ensevelie pour rechercher ce qui restait. Un riche marchand, Publius Cornelius Teges, avait une belle copie d'une statue grecque réputée d'un éphèbe, jeune soldat grec, transformé en lampadaire tenant une lampe de la main droite. Il démonta cette statue et l'emmenait avec lui lorsqu'il fut asphyxié et enseveli sous le plafond de sa propre maison, connue aujourd'hui sous le nom de Maison de l'Éphèbe.

Die Pompejaner erfreuten sich nicht nur am Bemalen ihrer Wände, sondern sie liebten es auch, ihre Heimstätten mit Marmor- und Bronzestandbildern auszuschmücken. Diese Objekte besaßen so großen Wert für sie, daß sie so viele wie möglich auf ihre Flucht mitnahmen und zahlreiche Bewohner in die verschüttete Stadt zurückkehrten, um zu retten, was noch zu retten war. Ein reicher Händler, Publius Cornelius Teges, besaß eine schöne Kopie eines berühmten griechischen Standbildes eines Ephebos, streitbarer griechischer Jüngling in militärischer Staatserziehung, die als Lampenständer benutzt wurde, und zwar diente der rechte Arm der Statue als Träger von Öllampen. Dieser

Händler nun demontierte die Lampe aber, als er die Figur wegtrug, wurde er unter der Decke seines eigenen Hauses begraben, das heute als das Haus des Ephebos bekannt ist.

A tripod with legs of satyrs (from Herculaneum), now in Naples Museum.

Trépied à pieds de satyres (d'Herculanum), maintenant dans le Musée de Naples.

Dreifuß (aus Herculaneum), der von bronzenen Satyrn gehalten wird, jetzt im Museum zu Neapel.

The bronze figure of Apollo the Citherist, from the House of L. Popidi Secundi Augustiana (now in Naples Museum).

Figure en bronze d'Apollo le Joueur de cithare de la Maison de L. Popidi Secundi Augustiana (maintenant dans le Musée de Naples).

Das Bronzestandbild des Apollo der Kitharaspieler aus dem Hause des L. Popidi Secundi Augustiana (nun im Museum zu Neapel).

The atrium of a house on the Via dell'Abbondanza.

L'atrium d'une maison sur la Via dell'Abbondanza.

Das Atrium eines Hauses in der Via dell' Abbondanza.

Bronze bull in the House of Lucius Pontius. (The original is now in Naples Museum).

Taureau en bronze dans la Maison de Lucius Pontius. (L'original se trouve maintenant dans le Musée de Naples).

Bronzestier im Hause des Lucius Pontius. (Das Original befindet sich nun im Museum zu Neapel).

Figured capital from the House of the Bull with the bust of a Maenad (in the Antiquarium).

Chapiteau orné de figures de la Maison du Taureau avec le buste d'une Ménade (dans l'Antiquarium).

Ein mit Figuren geschmücktes Kapitell aus dem Hause des Stiers mit der Büste einer Mänade (im Antiquarium).

The luxurious and lavishly decorated House of the Vettii was owned by two rich merchants, Aulus Vettius Restitutus and Aulus Vettius Conviva. The hermae on the right are in the peristyle of the house.

La Maison des Vettii, luxueuse et décorée avec abandon, appartenait à deux riches marchands, Aulus Vettius Restitutus et Aulus Vettius Conviva. Les hermès à droite sont dans le péristyle de la maison.

Das luxuriöse und verschwenderisch geschmückte Haus der Vettier gehörte zwei reichen Händlern, Aulus Vettius Restitutus und Aulus Vettius Conviva. Die Hermen (rechts) befinden sich im Peristyl des Hauses.

Right and opposite: Marble and bronze figures in the peristyle of the House of the Vettii.

A droite et sur page en face: Statues en marbre et en bronze dans le péristyle de la Maison des Vettii.

Rechts und gegenüber: Statuen aus Marmor und Bronze im Peristyl des Hauses der Vettier.

All these figures from the House of the Vettii contain fountain-jets. When these and the other fountains are turned on amongst the roses in the garden one can see and hear how agreeably the Vettii had adorned their home.

Toutes ces statues dans la Maison des Vettii contiennent des jets d'eau. Lorsque ceux-ci et d'autres fontaines dans le jardin jaillissent parmi les roses, il est possible de voir et d'entendre la façon dont les Vettii avaient rendu leur maison belle.

All diese Figuren aus dem Hause der Vettier enthalten Springbrunnendüsen. Wenn diese und die andern Fontänen zwischen den Rosen des Gartens sprühen, ist es leicht möglich, sich die Schönheit und Lieblichkeit dieses Hauses vorzustellen.

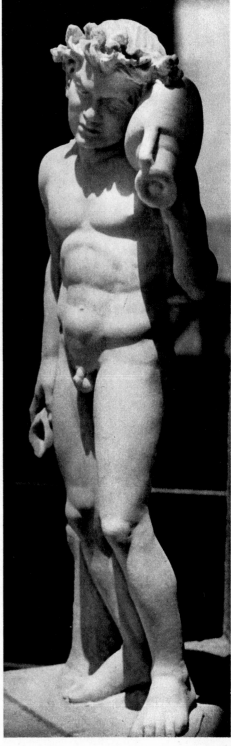

Paintings in the House of the Vettii. The Pompeiians delighted in depicting these little cupids either at play or engaged in all kinds of tasks.

Peintures dans la Maison des Vettii. Les Pompéiens adoraient montrer ces petits cupidons, soit jouant soit s'adonnant à maintes tâches.

Malereien im Hause der Vettier. Die Pompejaner erfreuten sich an der Darstellung dieser kleinen Cupidos, die entweder spielen oder verschiedenartige Arbeiten verrichten.

The painting in the lararium shows the genius of the paterfamilias between two Lares, household gods, with the serpent Agathodaimon about to accept the funeral offerings.

La peinture dans le lararium montre le génie du paterfamilias entre deux lares, dieux du foyer, avec le serpent Agathodaimon sur le point d'accepter les offres funéraires.

Die Malerei im Lararium zeigt den Genius des Paterfamilias zwischen zwei Laren, Hausgötter, mit der Schlange Agathodaimon, die im Begriffe ist, die dargebotenen Opfer anzunehmen.

The lararium in the House of the Cryptoporticus.

Le lararium dans la Maison du Cryptoporticus.

Das Lararium im Hause des Cryptoportikus.

The cryptoporticus (a subterranean passage),
which was sumptuously decorated.

Le cryptoporticus (passage souterrain) somp-
tueusement décoré.

Der Cryptoportikus (ein unterirdischer Gang),
der reich geschmückt war.

The inhabitants of the House of the Cryptoporticus took refuge from the eruption in
these underground apartments. Then they
broke out through one of the skylights but
collapsed in the garden above.

Les habitants de la Maison du Cryptoporticus
(Galerie Fermée) se refugièrent dans ces
appartements souterrains lors de l'éruption.
Puils ils s'échappèrent par une lucarne mais
moururent dans le jardin.

Die Bewohner des Hauses des Cryptoportikus
suchten in diesen unterirdischen Wohnungen
vor der Eruption Zuflucht. Dann brachen sie
durch eines der Oberlichter aus, doch starben
sie im Garten.

The Villa of the Mysteries. This country house, discovered outside the walls beyond the Herculaneum Gate, gives us a picture of one of those villas of which Pliny said were 'extremely thick upon that beautiful coast'. Within the city, town-houses looked inwards behind blind walls, but villas, surrounded by their terraced gardens, looked outwards over the sea and the countryside. The peristyle of the tufa columns *(below)* is enclosed by a low painted wall which hides the central garden.

La Villa des Mystères. Cette maison de campagne, retrouvée hors des murs au-delà de la Porta Herculano nous montre une de ces villas que Pline décrivait comme étant «fort nombreuses sur cette belle côte». Dans la ville les maisons étaient construites derrière de grands murs aveugles mais les villas, entourées de jardins en terrasses, s'ouvraient sur la mer et la campagne. Le péristyle des colonnes tuffeau *(dessous)* est encerclé par un mur peint, peu élevé, qui cache le jardin central.

Die Villa der Mysterien. Dieses Landhaus, das außerhalb der Stadtmauern nach der Porta Ercolano ausgegraben wurde, zeigt uns eine dieser Villen, von denen Plinius sagte, sie seien entlang dieser wunderbaren Küste außerordentlich dicht gesät. Innerhalb der Stadtmauern waren die Außenseiten der Häuser meist schmucklos, doch die Villen, von ihren terrassenförmig angelegten Gärten umgeben, waren nach außen gerichtet, gegen das Meer und die offene Landschaft. Das Peristyl der Tuffstein-Säulen *(unten)* ist von einer niederen bemalten Mauer umfaßt, die den mittleren Garten verdeckt.

On both sides of the atrium a corridor links the atrium with the porticoed verandas on the north and south of the house.

De chaque côté de l'atrium un couloir le relie aux vérandas à portiques au nord et au sud de la maison.

Auf beiden Seiten des Atriums verbindet ein Gang die mit Säulen umgebenen Veranden im Norden und im Süden des Hauses.

The corridor leading from the atrium to the northern portico.

Le couloir menant de l'atrium au portique nord.

Der Gang, der vom Atrium zum nördlichen Portikus führt.

Right: The tetrastyle atrium.

A droite: L'atrium tétrastyle.

Rechts: Das viersäulige Atrium.

The Villa of the Mysteries was begun in the third century B.C. but received several later additions. The original entrance on the east of the house opened on to a passage leading to the peristyle.

La Villa des Mystéres fut construite d'abord au troisième siècle av. J.C., mais elle fut agrandie plusieurs fois par la suite. L'entrée originale à l'est de la maison avait un passage menant au péristyle.

Die Villa der Mysterien wurde im dritten Jahrhundert v.Chr. erbaut, doch erhielt sie später verschiedene Erweiterungen. Der ursprüngliche Eingang auf der Ostseite des Hauses hatte einen Gang, der zum Peristyl führte.

Opposite: The small atrium.

En face: Le petit atrium.

Gegenüber: Das kleine Atrium.

A statue of Livia, wife of the emperor Augustus, which was found in the Villa of the Mysteries (now in Naples Museum). The gap below the head-covering shows where the portrait-head was added to a formal statue of a priestess.

Une statue de Livia, femme de l'Empereur Auguste, qui fut trouvée dans la Villa des Mystères (maintenant au Musée de Naples). L'espace endessous du revêtement de la tête montre l'endroit où la tête peinte fut ajoutée ensuite à une statue formelle d'une prêtresse.

Ein Standbild der Livia, Gattin des Kaisers Augustus, das in der Villa der Mysterien gefunden wurde (nun im Museum zu Neapel). Die Spalte unterhalb der Kopfbedeckung zeigt die Stelle auf, an welcher der Kopf auf die ehemalige Statue einer Priesterin gefügt wurde.

One of the most exciting discoveries in Pompeii was this painted room in the Villa of the Mysteries, which gives the house its name. It depicts in general terms the significance of the Dionysiac cult with special reference to a marriage. The centre of the composition, on the back wall, is a group of Dionysus and his bride Ariadne, flanked by satyrs and female attendants, one of whom is veiling or unveiling an enormous phallus.

L'une des plus émouvantes découvertes faite à Pompei fut cette chambre peinte dans la Villa des Mystères, qui donna son nom a la maison. En résumé, elle décrit la signification du culte de Dionisus avec des allusions particulières au mariage. Le centre de la composition sur le mur du fond est un groupe avec Dionisus et son épouse, entouré par des satyres et des servantes, dont l'une d'entre elles cache ou montre un énorme phallus.

Einer der aufregendsten Entdeckungen in Pompeji war dieser bemalte Raum in der Villa der Mysterien, welcher dem Haus den Namen verleiht. Diese Malereien zeigen, allgemein gesehen, die Bedeutung des Dionysoskultes und weist speziell auf eine Heirat hin. Die Mitte der Komposition, an der hinteren Wand, besteht aus einer Gruppe von Dionysos und seiner Braut Ariadne, die von Satyrn und weiblicher Dienerschaft, von denen eine einen großen Phallus entweder verschleiert oder entschleiert, flankiert ist.

The Dionysiac rites were secret and are not represented here in any detail. On the left of the entry is the seated figure of the bride's mother, and on the opposite side is her daughter arraying herself for the wedding ceremony. Beyond the mother a heavily draped young woman walks meditatively towards the centre of the scene. She is thought to represent the mother's memory of herself at her own wedding, years previously. Beyond, a naked boy reads from a ritual scroll with the help of a seated woman who points to the text with a stylus. Next, a young woman with an olive-leaf crown carries a dish bearing unidentifiable objects towards a priestess who, with two assistants, is carrying out an act of lustration appropriate to the beginning of an act of worship. Next there is Papposilenus playing on his lyre, then a young pan playing his pipes, with a panisca suckling a kid. Then an awestruck woman heralds the god and his associates on the end-wall. Between the woman and Dionysus is Silenus with two satyrs engaged upon a ceremony of which the meaning is doubtful. Beyond the central group, not illustrated, a young woman is being scourged by a winged demon, perhaps (it has been suggested) as a warning for good behaviour!

Les rites Dionisiens étaient secrets et aucun detail n'y fait allusion. A la gauche de l'entrée la représentation assise de la mère de la mariée et de l'autre coté sa fille se parant pour la cérémonie du mariage. Derrière la mère, une jeune femme lourdement drapée se dirige méditativement vers le centre de la scène. Elle est supposée représenter la mémoire de la mère à son propre mariage, des années auparavant. Derrière, un jeune garcon lit un rouleau de papier rituel aidé d'une femme assise qui montre le texte avec un stilet. Ensuite, une jeune femme avec une couronne de feuilles d'olivier porte une coupe dans laquelle se trouvent des objets non-identifiés à une prêtresse qui, avec deux assistants, est en train d'exécuter un acte de lustration approprié à un acte d'adoration. Ensuite se succèdent Papposilenus jouant sur sa lyre, un jeune Pan jouant de la flûte et une panisca allaitant un chevreau. Ensuite une femme terrifiée annonçant le Dieu et ses associés sur le mur du fond. Entre la femme et Dionysus, Silenus avec deux satyres est occupé à une cérémonie dont le sens est incertain. Derrière le groupe central, non representée, une jeune femme est fouettée par un demon ailé, peut-être (il a été suggéré) comme mise en garde pour un bon comportement.

Die Dionysosriten waren geheim und sind hier nicht in Einzelheiten dargestellt. Links vom Eingang ist die sitzende Figur der Brautmutter, und an der gegenüberliegenden Seite bereitet sich die Tochter für die Hochzeitszeremonien vor. Eine junge Frau, in schwere Falten gehüllt, schreitet neben der Mutter nachdenklich auf die Mitte der Szene zu. Man nimmt an, daß sie die Erinnerung der Mutter an ihre eigene Hochzeit, die Jahre zuvor stattfand, darstellt. Daneben ist ein nakter Knabe, der mit Hilfe einer Frau, die sitzend den Text mit einem Zeigestock anzeigt, von einer rituellen Papyrusrolle vorliest. Als nächstes sehen wir ein junges Weib, mit einer Krone aus Olivenblättern, die eine mit undefinierbaren Gegenständen gefüllte Platte zu einer Priesterin trägt, die mit zwei Gehilfen damit beschäftigt ist, eine Reinigungszeremonie, die dem Beginn einer Andacht entspricht, zu vollbringen. Daneben ist Papposilenos, der seine Leier spielt, dann ein junger Pan seine Panflöte spielend, und eine Panisca, die ein Zicklein stillt. An der letzten Wand sehen wir eine von Ehrfurcht ergriffene Frau, die dem Erscheinen Gottes und seiner Gesellen beiwohnt. Zwischen den Frauen und Dionysos ist Silenos mit zwei Satyren, die mit einer Zeremonie beschäftigt sind, deren Sinn zweifelhaft ist. Hinter der Hauptgruppe (nicht illustriert), wird eine junge Frau von einem Dämon mit Flügeln gepeitscht, vielleicht (so wurde gesagt) als eine Warnung für gutes Betragen.

A statue of Hercules (in Naples Museum).

Une statue d'Hercules (au Musée de Naples).

Ein Standbild des Herkules (im Museum zu Neapel).

Right: A bronze statue of Dionysus (in the Antiquarium).

A droite: Une statue en bronze de Dionysos (dans l'Antiquarium).

Rechts: Eine Bronzestatue des Dionysos (im Antiquarium).

Left: The sepulchral exedra of the Priestess Mamia on the Via dei Sepolcri. Behind is the round temple of the Mausoleum of the Istacidii, probable owners of the Villa of the Mysteries.

A gauche: La salle de réunion sépulcrale (exedra) de la Prêtresse Mamia sur la Via dei Sepolcri. Derrière on voit le temple rond de la Mausolée de l'Istacidii, probablement les propriétaires de la Villa des Mystères.

Links: Das Grabmal der Priesterin Mamia auf der Via dei Sepolcri. Dahinter der runde Tempel des Mausoleums der Istacidii, wahrscheinliche Besitzer der Villa der Mysterien.

A funerary figure on the Via dei Sepolcri.

Figure funéraire sur la Via dei Sepolcri.

Trauernde Figur auf der Via dei Sepolcri.

Right: The tomb of the Aedile Vestorius Priscus.

A droite: Le tombeau de l'Edile Vestorius Priscus.

Rechts: Das Grab des Ädils Vestorius Priscus.

Tombs of the necropolis outside the Porta Nuceria.

Tombeaux de la nécropole qui se trouvent au-delà de la Porta Nuceria.

Gräber der Necropolis außerhalb der Porta Nuceria.

A wall painting in one of the Pompeiian necropoles.

Peinture sur un mur dans une des nécropoles de Pompéi.

Eine Wandmalerei in einer Necropolis von Pompeji.

Herculaneum
Herculanum

House of the Gem, and House of the Relief of Telephus, with the houses of modern Resina standing over them.

La Maison de la Gemme et la Maison du Relief de Telephus, avec les maisons de Resina au-dessus d'elles.

Haus der Gemme und Haus des Reliefs des Telephus, mit den Häusern von Resina darüber.

Herculaneum, according to legend, was founded by Hercules on his return from Spain. Its history is similar to that of Pompeii: an Oscan settlement, a Greek city, a Samnite conquest, an opponent Rome in the Social War, and finally a Roman colony.

Although excavations have not proceeded far enough to give a clear idea of the city's extent, its situation on a promontory between two fast-flowing streams limited expansion. It was probably about a third the size of Pompeii with only a quarter of the population.

Herculaneum was a quieter, more leisurely town than Pompeii. The streets do not have the deep wheel ruts made by heavy traffic or the stepping-stones for crossing busy roads. There are no signs of the posters and election propaganda which cover so many walls in Pompeii.

Herculaneum's position did not give it a natural harbour and it did not become a trading centre of any importance, nor, as far as we can tell from that part of the city so far uncovered, was there much industry; what workshops there are were used for luxury trades, the artisans worked largely to cater for the day-to-day needs of the community and, to judge by the amount of rope and tackle found, fishing was popular. The houses, were often of more than one storey; sometimes a floor was added in the Roman period to a Samnite house, showing a more advanced stage of development than in Pompeii. There is a bigger contrast here between the richer homes and the modest dwellings of the artisans. Along the edge of the promontory overlooking the sea the houses have gardens and terraces so arranged as to make the most of the view, and they have

more the atmosphere of a country house. In the area near the Palaestra, on the other hand, there is a large block of apartments or tenements of the kind found in the Roman port of Ostia.

In Pompeii roofs caved in with the weight of falling ash but in Herculaneum the volcanic mud flowed through and filled up every space leaving the roofs and upper storeys in position where they had not offered too much resistance to its passage. Here, by careful excavation, it has been possible to preserve the houses almost as they stood.

Overleaf right: The West Portico and buildings of the Great Palaestra. The Palaestra was larger than usual for the size of the town. It included a large hall for meetings and a big, cross-shaped swimming pool in the centre.

Herculanum, d'après la légende, fut fondé par Hercules après son retour d'Espagne. Son histoire est semblable à celle de Pompéi: colonie osque, cité grecque, conquête samnite, révolte contre Rome dans la Guerre Sociale et finalement colonie romaine. Bien que les fouilles ne soient pas encore suffisantes pour donner une idée nette de l'étendue de la cité, sa situation sur un promontoire entre deux fleuves rapides limita son expansion. La ville était probablement trois fois moins grande que Pompéi et avec un quart de sa population. Herculanum était une ville plus tranquille, moins bousculée que Pompéi. Les rues n'y ont pas les rigoles profondes faites par les roues des charrettes ni les pierres de gué pour traverser les rues commerçantes. Il n'y a pas trace d'enseignes et d'affiches électorales qui recouvrent tant de murs à Pompéi.

La situation d'Herculanum ne lui donnait pas de port naturel et la ville ne devint jamais un centre commercial important, ni, autant que nous puissions le voir dans la partie de la ville déjà excavée, y avait-il beaucoup d'industrie: les ateliers étaient pour des articles de luxe, les artisans travaillant surtout pour les besoins journaliers de la communauté, et, à en juger par toutes les cordes et articles de pêche qui y furent trouvés, la pêche était un sport favori.

Les maisons avient souvent plus d'un étage; parfois un étage ajouté à l'époque romaine sur une maison samnite montre un développement plus avancé qu'à Pompéi. Il y a plus de contraste ici entre les maisons plus riche et les habitations modestes des artisans. Sur la côté du promontoire, surplombant la mer, les maisons ont des jardins et des terrasses disposés de façon à profiter de la vue; elles ressemblent davantage aux villas. Près de Palestre il y a un grand bloc d'appartements comme on en a trouvé dans le port romain d'Ostia.

A Pompéi les toits s'effondrèrent sous le poids de la cendre, mais à Herculanum la boue volcanique déferla et s'infiltra partout laissant les toits et les étages en place lorsqu'il n'y avait pas de résistance. Ici, en fouillant avec soin, il a été possible de préserver les maisons presque intactes.

A droite: La Portique Ouest et les bâtiments du Grand Palestre. Ce gymnase étaite plus grand que ceux que l'on trouvait normalement dans une ville de cette importance. Il comprenait une grande salle pour des réunions et une grande piscine cruciforme au milieu.

scheideneren Heimstätten der Handwerker. Auf dem nach dem Meer gerichteten Hügelhang sind die Gärten und Terrassen der Häuser so angeordnet, daß die schönste Aussicht eingefangen wird und sie gleichen eigentlich eher Villen. In der Nähe der Palaestra gibt es große Wohnungsblöcke wie jene, die im römischen Hafen von Ostia gefunden wurden. In Pompeji stürzten die Dächer durch das Gewicht der fallenden Asche ein, doch über Herculaneum wälzte sich eine Lawine, bedeckte die Dächer, quoll in Fenster und Türen, füllte die Räume vollständig aus und ließ so die Dächer und Obergeschosse, wo diese ihnen keinen zu großen Widerstand bereitet hatten, unbeschädigt. Hier war es dank sorgfältiger Ausgrabung möglich, die Häuser in ihrem ursprünglichen Zustand zu erhalten.

Rechts: Der westliche Portikus und Gebäude der Großen Palaestra. Die Palaestra war größer als gewöhnlich für eine Stadt dieser Ordnung. Sie umfaßte eine weite Halle für Versammlungen und ein großes, in Kreuzform erbautes Schwimmbecken in der Mitte.

Herculaneum wurde, so erzählt die Legende, von Herkules nach seiner Rückkehr von Spanien gegründet. Seine Geschichte deckt sich mit jener Pompejis: eine Oskersiedlung, eine griechische Stadt, eine samnitische Eroberung, ein Aufstand gegen Rom während des Bundesgenossenkrieges, und schließlich eine römische Kolonie.

Obwohl die Ausgrabungen noch nicht weit genug fortgeschritten sind, um eine genaue Übersicht über die Ausdehnung der Stadt zu geben, ist gewiß, daß eine Expansion durch die Lage auf einer Erhebung zwischen zwei Strömen begrenzt wurde. Es hatte ungefähr ein Drittel der Größe Pompejis mit nur einem Viertel der Bevölkerung.

Herculaneum war eine ruhigere, müßigere Stadt als Pompeji. Die Straßen weisen nicht die tiefen Spuren von Wagenrädern auf, die bei regem Verkehr verursacht werden, und sie besitzen keine Schrittstufen zum Überqueren der verkehrsreichen Straßen. Es gibt keine Spuren von Anschlägen und Wahlslogans, die so viele Mauern in Pompeji bedecken.

Herculaneum besaß keinen natürlichen Hafen und diese Stadt wurde weder ein Handelszentrum von einiger Bedeutung noch, so weit wir nach dem bis jetzt freigelegten Teil der Stadt sagen können, gab es dort viel Industrie: die vorhandenen Werkstätten dienten Luxusgewerben, die Handwerker arbeiteten größtenteils, um für die täglichen Bedürfnisse der Gemeinschaft zu sorgen und, nach der beträchtlichen Zahl der gefundenen Seile und Fischereiartikel zu urteilen, war Fischfang ein beliebter Sport.

Die Häuser, von denen viele mehr als ein Stockwerk besaßen — manchmal wurde ein Stockwerk im römischen Stil auf ein samnitisches Haus gebaut —, zeigten ein fortgeschrittenes Entwicklungsstadium als in Pompeji. Es gibt hier einen größeren Gegensatz zwischen den reicheren Häusern und den be-

The houses of modern Resina are built directly over the main area of Herculaneum. Excavated here is the western portico of the Palaestra and its northern loggia. Passages through the solid rock on the right enable visitors to see parts of the cruciform swimming-pool in the centre of the Palaestra.

Les maisons de Resina, la ville moderne, sont construites directement au-dessus du centre d'Herculanum. Ici on voit les fouilles de la portique ouest du gymnase et la loggia du nord. Des passages à même le roc à droite permettent aux visiteurs de voir une partie de la piscine au centre du Palestre.

Die Häuser des modernen Resina wurden

direkt über dem Hauptteil Herculaneums erbaut. Diese Abbildung zeigt die Ausgrabungen des westlichen Portikus der Palaestra und ihre nördliche Loggia. Gänge durch den harten Fels ermöglichen den Besuchern, Teile des kreuzförmig erbauten Schwimmbeckens im Zentrum der Palaestra zu bewundern.

The atrium of the House of the Relief of Telephus. Between the pillars of the colonnade hang marble oscilla or masks and satirical figures.

L'atrium de la Maison du Relief de Telephus. Entre les piliers de la colonnade pendent des oscilles en marbre, sculptés sous forme de masques et de figures satiriques.

Das Atrium des Hauses des Reliefs des Telephus. Zwischen den Säulen der Kolonnade hängen marmorne Oscilla, die mit Masken und satirischen Gestalten geschmückt sind.

An oscillum carved with the heads of a Pan and a satyr, from the House of the Relief of Telephus.

Un oscille sculpté avec les têtes de Pan et d'un Satyr, de la Maison du Relief de Telephus.

Ein Oscillum, das mit den Köpfen eines Pan und eines Satyrs verziert ist, aus dem Hause des Reliefs des Telephus.

Reliefs, now in the House of Telephus. These reliefs have been composed from fragments found in this and other houses in the street. With others, now in museums overseas, they probably came from a public building in the centre of the city and were swept here by the flow of laval mud.

Des reliefs, maintenant dans la Maison de Telephus. Ces reliefs proviennent de fragments trouvés dans la maison et ailleurs dans la même rue. Avec d'autres reliefs que l'on trouve dans des musées outre-mer, ils ont dû venir d'un immeuble public au centre de la ville et être amené ici par le flot de boue et de lave.

Reliefs, nun im Hause des Telephus. Diese Reliefs wurden aus Fragmenten, die in diesem und anderen Häusern der Straße gefunden wurden, zusammengesetzt. Diese und andere Reliefs, die sich heute in überseeischen Museen befinden, stammten wahrscheinlich aus einem öffentlichen Gebäude im Zentrum der Stadt und wurden durch den Schlammstrom hierher geschwemmt.

The garden of the House of the Deer, looking from the summer triclinium. Before the eruption this terrace was on the edge of a promontory, and beyond the pergola would have been a panorama of sea and sky.

Two groups of deer attacked by hounds, one of which is illustrated, the figure of a satyr with a wineskin, and other statues now displayed in this house, were found in the garden.

Le jardin de la Maison du Cerf, vue du triclinium d'été. Avant l'éruption cette terrasse se trouvait au bord d'un promontoire, et la pergola devait donner vue sur la mer et le ciel. On a trouvé dans le jardin deux groupes de cerfs attaqués par des chiens (l'un illustré ici)

une statue de satyr avec une outre et d'autres encore qui se trouvent maintenant dans cette maison.

Der Garten des Hauses des Hirsches, vom Sommer-Triclinium aus gesehen. Vor der Eruption befand sich diese Terrasse auf dem Kamm eines Vorgebirges und die Pergola gewährte einen wunderbaren Blick auf Meer und Himmel.

Zwei Statuengruppen von Hirschen, die von Hunden angegriffen werden, (eine hier abgebildet), die Figur eines Satyrs mit einem Weinschlauch sowie andere Statuen, die nun in diesem Haus aufgestellt sind, wurden im Garten gefunden.

The house of the Wooden Partition. This patrician house is one of the most complete examples of a private home in Herculaneum or Pompeii. Left is the atrium, looking through the tablinium to the garden. The exceptional discovery in the House of the Wooden Partition is the screen of three double-leaved doors (the centre one missing) which gives the house its name. It closed off the tablinium, turning it into a separate reception room.

La Maison à la Cloison en Bois. Cette maison d'un patricien est un des exemples les mieux préservés d'une maison particulière à Herculanum ou à Pompéi. A gauche l'atrium, en regardant par le tablinum vers le jardin. Une découverte exceptionnelle faite dans cette Maison à la Cloison en Bois est un ensemble de trois portes à doubles battants (celui du milieu manque) qui donne son nom à la maison. Cette porte permettait d'isoler le tablinum pour en faire une salle de réception séparée.

Das Haus der Hölzernen Scheidewand. Dieses Patrizierhaus ist eines der besterhaltenen Beispiele eines Privathauses in Herculaneum oder Pompeji. Links ist das Atrium, mit Blick durch das Tablinum in den Garten. Die außergewöhnliche Entdeckung in dem Haus der Hölzernen Scheidewand besteht in der Zwischenwand aus drei Doppelflügeltüren (die mittlere fehlt), nach der das Haus benannt wird. Es schließt das Tablinum ab und verwandelte es so in einen separaten Empfangsraum.

The atrium looking outwards to the street.

L'atrium — en regardant vers la rue.

Das Atrium mit Blick auf die Straße.

The frames of two beds in the House of the Wooden Partition.

Les cadres de deux lits trouvés dans la Maison à la Cloison en Bois

Zwei Bettgestelle im Hause der Hölzernen Scheidewand.

Left: a table of 'fior di pesco' marble supported by a figure of the Phrygian god Attis, found on the upper floor of the house.

A gauche: Une table en marbre «fior di pesco» soutenue par une figure d'Attis, le dieux phrygien, qui fut trouvée au premier étage.

Links: Ein Tisch aus „fior di pesco" Marmor, der durch eine Statue des phrygischen Gottes Attis getragen wird, der im Obergeschoß des Hauses gefunden wurde.

Right: The House of the Great Portal. The brick half-columns, which were originally stuccoed and painted red, have capitals carved with winged victories.

A droite: La Maison du Grand Portail. Les demi-colonnes en briques, qui étaient recouvertes de stuc et peintes en rouge, sont sculptées avec des victoires ailées.

Rechts: Das Haus des Großen Portals. Die Halbsäulen aus Backstein, die ursprünglich stukkiert und rot bemalt waren, besitzen Kapitelle, die mit beflügelten Siegesgöttinnen verziert sind.

The nymphaeum in the House of the Mosaic of Neptune and Amphitrite, decorated with glass paste mosaics, from which the house takes its name. A nymphaeum was a kind of grotto dedicated to the nymphs, and naturally included a pool or fountain.

Le nymphaeum de la Maison des Mosaïques de Neptune et d'Amphitrite; orné de mosaïques en verre qui donnent le nom à la maison. Le nymphaeum était un genre de grotte voué aux nymphes et naturellement il y avait une piscine ou fontaine.

Das Nymphaeum im Hause des Mosaiks des Neptuns und der Amphitrite, mit Glaspastemosaiken geschmückt, nach denen das Haus benannt wurde. Ein Nymphaeum war eine Art Grotte, den Nymphen zugeeignet, und natürlich einen Teich oder eine Fontäne enthielt.

Left: Wine amphorae in the shop which fronts the House of the Mosaic of Neptune and Amphitrite.

A gauche: Amphore de vin dans un magasin devant la Maison des Mosaïques de Neptune et d'Amphitrite.

Links: Weinamphoren im Laden, gegenüber dem Hause des Mosaiks des Neptuns und der Amphitrite.

Right: a small nymphaeum in the House of the Skeleton, with the central niche depicting the face of a female goddess rising out of acanthus leaves.

A droite: Un petit nymphaeum dans la Maison du Squelette avec une niche centrale montrant la face d'une déesse émergeante des feuilles d'acanthe.

Rechts: Ein kleines Nymphaeum im Hause des Skeletts, mit der Mittelnische, auf der das Antlitz einer Göttin abgebildet ist, die aus Akanthusblättern aufsteigt.

The lararium in the garden of the House of the Carbonised Furniture.
Right: A wooden triclinium couch in the House.

Le lararium dans le jardin de la Maison des Meubles Carbonisés.
A droite: Un lit triclinium en bois dans la maison.

Das Lararium im Garten des Hauses der Verkohlten Möbel.
Rechts: Ein hölzernes Triclinium-Ruhebett des Hauses.

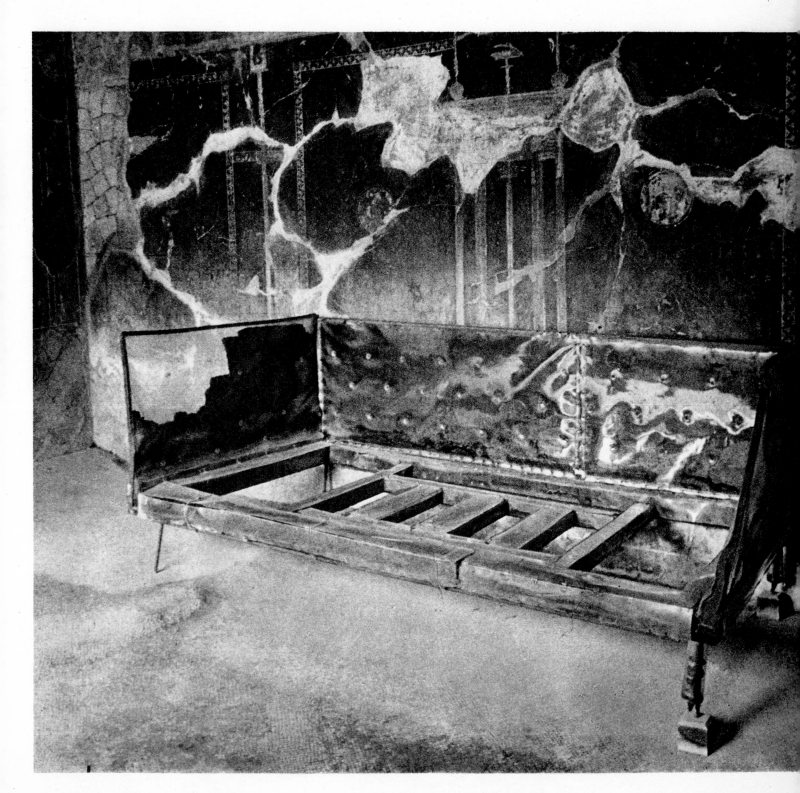

Left: The Apodyterium of the Women's Baths. The pavement mosaic shows a large riton. Here the women would have left their clothes.

A gauche: L'apodyterium (vestiare des bains pour les femmes). La mosaïque sur le sol montre un grand triton. Les femmes se déshabillaient ici.

Links: Das Apodyterium in den Frauenbädern. Der Mosaikboden zeigt einen großen Triton. Hier konnten die Frauen ihre Gewänder zurücklassen.

Right: The tepidarium of the Women's Baths, with the apodyterium beyond.

A droite: Le tepidarium. L'apodyterium se trouve au fond.

Rechts: Das Tepidarium in den Frauenbädern, mit dem Apodyterium dahinter.

Left: The Decumanus Maximus, the main street. This is the northern extremity of the present excavations. It probably adjoined the Forum which is still buried under the houses of Resina. This street, the widest in Herculaneum, was closed to wheeled traffic.

A gauche: Decumanus Maximus, la rue principale. Elle se trouve à l'extrême nord des fouilles actuelles. Probablement voisine du Forum qui est encore enseveli sous des maisons de Resina. Cette rue, la plus large d'Herculanum, était réservée aux piétons.

Links: Decumanus Maximus, die Hauptstraße. Hier sehen wir den nördlichen Abschluß der gegenwärtigen Ausgrabungen. Sie lief wahrscheinlich zum Forum, das noch immer unter den Häusern von Resina verschüttet ist. Diese Straße, die breiteste in ganz Herculaneum, war dem Verkehr geschlossen.

Right: The chapel of the College of the Priests of Augustus on the Decumanus Maximus. A painting of Hercules with Juno and Minerva is on the left-hand wall of the chapel.

A droite: La chapelle du Collège des Prêtres d'Auguste, sur le Decumanus Maximus. Une peinture d'Hercules avec Junon et Minerve se trouve sur le mur de gauche de la chapelle.

Rechts: Der Tempel des Kollegiums der Augustalen, auf dem Decumanus Maximus. Eine Malerei des Herkules mit Juno und Minerva befindet sich auf der linken Mauer des Tempels.

Next to the College of the Priests of Augustus
there is a house with this beautiful decoration
on a vaulted tablinum.

A côté du Collège des Prêtres d'Auguste se
trouve cette maison avec une belle décoration
dans le tablinum (galerie) voûté.

Neben dem Kollegium der Augustalen befindet sich ein Haus mit dieser wunderbaren
Verzierung auf einem gewölbten Tablinum.

Right: A wooden grill, preserved for nearly two thousand years, now behind glass.

A droite: Une grille en bois, préservée pendant près de deux milles ans. Maintenant sous verre.

Rechts: Ein hölzernes Gitterwerk, während fast zweitausend Jahren erhalten, nun unter Glas.

Left: The atrium and tablinum of a house in insula V.

A gauche: L'atrium et le tablinum d'une maison dans l'insula V.

Links: Das Atrium und das Tablinum eines Hauses in Insula V.

Left and below: A balance-scale, a lantern, lamps and weights, discovered in various places in Herculaneum.

A gauche et en-dessous: Une balance, une lanterne, des lampes et des poids, découverts dans Herculanum.

Links und unten: Eine Waagschale, eine Laterne, Lampen und Gewichtsteine, die in verschiedenen Orten in Herculaneum gefunden wurden.

A wooden cupboard, possibly a shrine, in an upstairs room of the House of the Bicentenary. A cross appears to have been inserted into a stuccoed panel above the shrine. This may have been a private Christian oratory, and if so, it is the earliest indication of the cult of the cross in Christian worship.

Une armoire en bois, peut-être un autel, dans une des chambres au premier étage de la Maison du Bicentenaire. Une croix semble avoir été ajoutée dans le panneau en stuc au-dessus de l'autel. Peut-être un oratoire chrétien privé. Si ceci est le cas, c'est la première indication du culte de la croix dans l'adoration chrétienne.

Ein hölzerner Schrank, möglicherweise ein Altarschrein, in einem Raum des Obergeschosses des Hauses des Bizentenars.
Ein Kreuz scheint in eine stukkierte Tafel oberhalb des Schreines eingesetzt gewesen zu sein. Dies könnte ein privates christliches Oratorium gewesen sein. In diesem Falle ist es der früheste Hinweis auf den Kreuzeskult in der christlichen Gottesverehrung.

The back room of a jeweller's shop adjoining the Palaestra. There is a small loom on the right, and on the remains of the elegantly veneered bed lie the bones of a young man.

Une salle derrière un magasin de bijoutier près du Palestre. Un petit métier à droite; sur l'élégant lit en bois verni les os d'un jeune homme.

Der Hinterraum eines Schmuckgeschäftes, bei der Palaestra. Zur Rechten gibt es einen Webstuhl und auf den Überresten eines elegant furnierten Bettes liegen die Knochen eines jungen Mannes.

The entrance-hall of the suburban baths, built outside the town-walls below the House of the Gem and the House of the Deer. They are one of the best preserved bathing-establishments of the Flavian period. The hall is lit by a skylight above four columns, suggesting a small tetrastyle atrium. Beneath the columns of the entrance hall, a fine bronze herm of Apollo forms a fountain from which water flows into the marble bowl and then into the impluvium basin.

L'entrée des bains qui se trouvaient hors de la ville sous la Maison de la Gemme et la Maison du Cerf. C'est l'établissement des bains le mieux préservé de l'époque Flavienne. L'entrée est éclairée par une lucarne au-dessus de quatre colonnes, évoquant un petit atrium tétrastyle. Sous les colonnes de l'entrée, une statue en bronze d'Apollon forme une fontaine d'où l'eau jaillit dans un bassin en marbre pour passer dans l'impluvium.

Die Eingangshalle der vorstädtischen Thermen, die vor den Toren der Stadt unterhalb des Hauses der Gemme und des Hauses des Hirsches erbaut wurden. Es handelt sich um eine der besterhaltenen Badeanlagen der flavischen Periode. Die Halle wird durch ein oberhalb vier Säulen liegendes Oberlicht beleuchtet, was den Eindruck eines kleinen viersäuligen Atriums erweckt. Unterhalb der Säulen der Eingangshalle bildet eine schöne Bronzeherme des Apollo einen Springbrunnen, dessen Wasser sich in die Marmorschale und anschließend in das Impluvium ergießt.

Left: The original wooden door is still in place resting on a block of solidified lava.

Below: The rooms of the suburban baths are decorated with marble and fine stucco work.

A gauche: La porte originale en bois est encore en place, reposant sur un bloc de lave solidifiée.

En dessous: Les salles des établissements de bains hors de la ville étaient richement ornées de marbre et de stuc.

Links: Die Originalholztür steht noch an ihrem Platz und ruht auf einem Block aus erstarrter Lava.

Unten: Die Räume der vorstädtischen Thermen sind mit Marmor und schöner Stuckarbeit verziert.

Outside Herculaneum, to the west, was a palatial villa which, despite a second burial under a stratum of lava from the 1631 eruption of Vesuvius, was partially explored in the eighteenth century. It was named the Villa of the Papyri from the extensive library of philosophical works, written on papyrus, which was discovered there. Poisonous vapours forced the tunellers to abandon the site in 1765, but not before the library and a fine collection of sculpture had been removed from the area of the peristyle and garden, of which the bronzes on these and the following three pages form a part. They are now in the National Museum at Naples.

En dehors de la ville d'Herculanum, vers l'ouest, se trouvait une magnifique villa qui, en dépit du fait qu'elle fut ensevelie une deuxième fois sous une couche de lave lors de l'éruption du Vésuve en 1631, fut partiellement redécouverte au dix-huitième siècle. Elle fut appellée la Villa des Papyrus à cause de la grande bibliothèque qui y fut découverte contenant des oeuvres philosophiques écrites sur papyrus. Des vapeurs toxiques obligèrent les excavateurs d'abandonner le site en 1765, mais seulement après que la bibliothèque et une magnifique collection de sculptures aient été enlevées du péristyle et du jardin. Les bronzes illustrés sur les quatre pages qui suivent forment partie de cette collection. Ils sont maintenant dans le Musée National de Naples.

Außerhalb der Stadtmauern Herculaneums, im Westen, befand sich eine palastartige Villa, die, trotz einer zweiten Verschüttung unter einer Lavaschicht aus dem Vesuvausbruch des Jahres 1631, teilweise im achtzehnten Jahrhundert erforscht wurde. Sie wurde die Villa der Papyri genannt, nach der großen Bibliothek philosophischer Werke, auf Papyrusrollen geschrieben, die hier entdeckt wurden. Schwefeldämpfe zwangen die Ganggräber, die Stätte im Jahre 1765 zu verlassen, doch erst, nachdem die Bibliothek und eine wunderbare Sammlung von Skulpturen aus dem Gebiet des Peristyls und des Gartens weggeschafft worden war. Die auf dieser und den drei nachfolgenden Seiten gezeigten Bronzen bilden einen Teil dieser Sammlung.

Sie befinden sich nun im Nationalmuseum zu Neapel.

Bronze figures from the Villa of the Papyri.

Figures en bronze de la Villa des Papyrus.

Bronzefiguren aus der Villa der Papyri.

The earliest wall-painting in Pompeii and Herculaneum consists of simple dados and panels which frequently imitate marble, but after the formation of the Roman colonies elaborate architectural *trompe l'oeil* effects appear and small pictures are inserted between the architectural elements.
Subjects frequently portrayed the use of the room where they were painted: still-lifes of food in a dining room, erotic subjects in a bedroom, flowers in a garden peristyle. Paintings in shops and taverns reflected the everyday activities within them. Everywhere mythological subjects were popular.

Les plus anciennes peintures à Pompéi et à Herculanum sont des lambris et des panneaux qui imitent souvent le marbre; après la formation des colonies romaines, il y eut des effets trompe l'oeil compliqués et de petits tableaux furent insérés entre les éléments architecturaux.
Les sujets sont souvent des sujets naturels: des natures mortes de nourritures dans une salle à manger, des sujets érotiques dans une chambre à coucher, des fleurs dans un péristyle de jardin. Les peintures dans les magasins et tavernes reflétaient les activités journalières. Partout des sujets mythologiques foisonnaient.

Die frühesten Wandmalereien in Pompeji und Herculaneum sind einfache Wandbekleidungen und Tafeln, die oft Marmor imitieren, doch nach der Bildung der römischen Kolonien treten kunstvolle architektonische Raumdurchblicke auf und kleine Bilder werden zwischen die architektonischen Elemente eingefügt.
Die Räume der Häuser wurden häufig je nach ihrer Bestimmung passend bemalt: Stillleben mit Lebensmitteln in einem Eßzimmer, erotische Themen in einem Schlafzimmer, Blumen in einem Gartenperistyl. Malereien in Kaufläden und Tavernen geben Einblick in das dort herrschende Alltagstreiben. Mythologische Themen waren sehr beliebt.

Left: A portrait of a meditative young woman.

Below: Detail from a painting of Iphigenia in Aulis.

A gauche: Un portrait d'une jeune femme qui médite.

En dessous: Détail d'une peinture d'Iphigénie en Aulis.

Links: Ein Porträt einer meditativen jungen Frau.

Unten: Ausschnitt aus einer Malerei der Iphigenia auf Aulis.

The Three Graces.

Les Trois Grâces.

Die Drei Grazien.

The Rape of Europa.

Enlèvement d'Europa.

Der Raub der Europa.

Venus and Cupid.

Vénus et Cupidon.

Venus und Cupido.